The Voyage of Charles Darwin

His autobiographical writings selected and arranged
by Christopher Ralling

MAYFLOWER BOOKS
NEW YORK

Library of Congress Cataloging in Publication Data

Darwin, Charles Robert, 1809–1882.
  The voyage of Charles Darwin.

  Includes index.
    1. Darwin, Charles Robert, 1809–1882. 2. Naturalists—England—
Biography. I. Ralling, Christopher. II. Title
QH31.D2A25 1979   575'0092'4 [B]   79–916
ISBN 0–8317–9212–4
Manufactured in Great Britain

First American edition

The BBC TV/Time-Life television series *The Voyage of Charles Darwin* is
produced by Christopher Ralling, with Ned Kelly as natural history
director and Martyn Friend as drama director, and written by Robert
Reid. The main characters are played as follows: Charles Darwin,
Malcolm Stoddard; Captain FitzRoy, Andrew Burt; Lieutenant
Wickham, David Ashton; Dr Robert Darwin, Iain Cuthbertson;
Thomas Huxley, Joseph Blatchley; Josiah Wedgwood, George Cole;
Emma Wedgwood, Cherith Mellor.

Contents

Introduction

Surprisingly, for such a reticent and private man, Charles Darwin wrote a great deal about himself. Equally surprisingly perhaps, considering his universal fame, this book represents the first attempt to put together a selection of his autobiographical writing in chronological order, and within the pages of a single volume. Like the BBC 2 Television Series it is not simply about a voyage round the World. It is also the voyage of a man's mind.

In selecting passages for the general reader we have had one great advantage which Darwin himself never enjoyed. Throughout the voyage of the *Beagle*, Darwin pursued many lines of thought, and expressed his interest in almost everything. But he had no idea at this stage of his life that his observations would gradually lead him to the theory of natural selection, and a permanent place among the world's great men of science. Today, however, it is possible to read both the Diary and the Journal, and see where his thoughts were beginning to lead him. These are the passages we have tended to concentrate on. In all cases we have regularised spelling, punctuation and place-names according to modern usage. Editorial contributions in the text, which have been kept to a minimum, are indicated by square brackets.

There are three main sources of material: the Autobiography, the Diary and the Journal. (The Journal was in effect the Diary rearranged by Darwin for publication, though with many omissions and additions.)

THE DIARY

Darwin's Diary was sent back to England in instalments for eventual collection in one volume. It was based on notes made in eighteen tiny pocketbooks which give us a vivid sense of the cramped life of the *Beagle*. The Diary was first published in full by his grand-daughter Nora Barlow, without whose pioneer work the present volume would have been impossible. Darwin used the pocketbooks for two purposes: as a daily record of events (which proved to be far from daily in practice), and also for more contemplative entries, which he must have worked at during the longer sea passages. It is surprising how many of the latter he was later able to transfer almost verbatim for publication in the Journal. There are very few personal remarks about his fellow shipmates, but whether that is a reflection on his own good nature, or apprehension that someone else on board might read them, it is difficult at this distance to say. One has to turn to the Autobiography, written many years later, for an accurate picture of the uneasy relationship between Darwin and FitzRoy during some parts of the voyage. In her Preface to the 1933 edition of the Diary, Nora Barlow quotes from a letter from Charles to his sisters towards the end of the voyage, in which he wrote that 'Captain FitzRoy proposed me to join him in publishing the account; that is for him to have the disposal and arranging of my Journal, and to mingle it with his own. Of course I have said I am perfectly willing, if he wants materials, or thinks the chit-chat details of my Journal are any ways worth publishing.' One can sense the disappointment he must have felt at that suggestion. He may even have resolved at the time to have nothing to do with it.

Even as a young man Darwin had a considerable ambition beneath his natural modesty. But it was difficult for him to argue with the captain of the ship, who had offered him the fantastic opportunity of going on the voyage in the first place. In the event, some time during the early months ashore the idea for mingling Darwin's journal with FitzRoy's got lost, or conveniently forgotten.

THE JOURNAL

In December 1836, after consulting a publisher named Colburn, FitzRoy wrote to Darwin suggesting that the Journal of the voyage should be published in three volumes. The first would contain Captain King's description of the first voyage of the *Beagle*, before Darwin joined the ship. The second would be FitzRoy's own narrative of the second voyage, and the third would be entirely Darwin's, writing as the official ship's naturalist. Profits, if any, would be equally divided. We do not know if anything had been said during the preceding months, but there was no further suggestion that FitzRoy would have the arranging of Darwin's material.

It was a fortunate decision. Darwin's volume was to achieve a far greater popularity than the other two, almost reaching the status of a Victorian best-seller. But, before publication, it very nearly became the cause of a permanent rift between the two men. Darwin sent FitzRoy a draft of his Introduction, which completely omitted the usual courtesies and acknowledgements. FitzRoy was furious. He sent a very stiff reply.

'I was also astonished at the total omission of any notice of the officers, either particular or general. My memory is rather tenacious respecting a variety of transactions in which you were concerned with them and others in the *Beagle*. Perhaps you were not aware that the ship which carried us safely was first employed in exploring and surveying, whose officers were not ordered to collect and were therefore at liberty to keep the best of all, nay all, their specimens for themselves. To their honour, they gave you the preference.'

Darwin was duly mortified. Indeed it seems strangely out of character for him to have made the omission in the first place. Whatever the truth, the incident reveals that the underlying tension and rivalry between the two men went remarkably deep. Nothing of that, of course, is to be found in the Journal itself. For years, FitzRoy's volume of the Journal remained in comparative obscurity. In fact it was not until David Stanbury published his excellent selection for the Folio Society in 1977 that the captain of the *Beagle* could be seen in his true colours. He was neither so pompous nor so verbose as we had been led to believe.

Nevertheless it is Darwin's Journal, containing as it does so many clues to his later development, which has become the classic. Considering he had few pretensions as a writer, it is a pleasure to read, even today. Some of the descriptive passages have a simple eloquence which suggests that the author could easily have made his living by the pen, had he not devoted the remainder of his life to natural history.

AUTOBIOGRAPHY

If any of those shocked Victorians who imagined Charles Darwin to be the devil incarnate had actually met the shy recluse nursing his ill-health at Down House, they might have found it hard to recognise their adversary. It took him twenty years before he could be persuaded to publish his findings on natural selection, and even then he was only goaded into writing *The Origin of Species* by the parallel research of another scientist, Alfred Wallace. Part of his reticence undoubtedly sprang from a dread of seeing his cherished theories ridiculed by some of his fellow scientists. But he also wanted to avoid upsetting the religious susceptibilities of his wife.

It was Emma, however, who finally persuaded him to write his Autobiography during the last five years of his life. He used to work at it for about an hour in the afternoons. Without it, we should have a much less clear idea of what his own religious beliefs were at the various stages of his life, from his undergraduate days when he was destined for the Church, to his final disillusionment. 'Disbelief crept over me at a very slow rate, but at last it was complete.' Apart from a few private letters, the Autobiography is also the only place where Darwin recorded his true relationship with FitzRoy; and only then some years after the latter had committed suicide.

In these days of intimate revelations it is hard to understand why the first publication of the Autobiography should have been the cause of a family row. When it finally appeared, 6000 words had been omitted, including all his references to religion and most of his comments on FitzRoy. It was Charles Darwin's grand-daughter Nora Barlow who published the first unexpurgated version of the Auto-biography in 1958. Her comments put the matter in proper per-spective.

'The family was, in fact, divided concerning the publication of some of the passages relating to Charles Darwin's religious beliefs. Francis, the editor, held the view that complete publication was the right course, whilst other members of the family felt strongly that Charles's views, so privately recorded and not intended for publica-tion, would be damaging to himself in their crudity.

'I write as one of the next generation, and it is difficult now to imagine the state of tension that existed in what had always seemed to us a solid and united phalanx of uncles and aunts. . . . Nevertheless it is clear that opinions were divided and feelings ran high in this united family, perhaps best explained by a divided loyalty amongst the children between the science of their father and the religion of their mother; though the differences of view that existed caused no estrangement between the parents.'

The fact that the whole Autobiography is not included in the present volume is entirely to do with reasons of space, and not censor-ship. At the beginning there is a long description of his father, which has been considerably shortened; and towards the end there is a list of the eminent men whom Darwin had met, or who had influenced him. This, too, has been curtailed to make room for more pertinent material.

Today, the majority of Christians no longer regard the discoveries of science as a direct threat to their faith, and it is difficult to under-stand why the publication of *The Origin of Species* in 1859 should have caused such a furore.

On the face of it, the theory of 'natural selection' among plants and animals does not appear to be particularly blasphemous or outrageous. Darwin himself was at pains to avoid applying his ideas to the origin of Man. He confined himself to one rather diffident sentence at the end of the book: 'In the distant future, I see open fields for far more important researches. Light will be thrown on the origin of Man, and his history.'

Nevertheless it was this aspect of the book, with all its implications, that his critics fastened upon. Man, they insisted, could not have been created in the image and likeness of God, and at the same time be descended from the apes. And so, for many Victorians, this very sick and private man, living the life of a near-recluse at his home in Kent, became a kind of monster. Was he actually saying that God resembled an ape? Was he daring to deny that, alone among all the forms of life on this planet, Man possessed an immortal soul? Darwin had been careful to say none of these things, but the conclusions were there to be drawn by others; and drawn they were. He was less concerned for himself than for his wife Emma. He knew that his own loss of faith was painful to her. In her own words, he 'seemed to be putting God further and further off'.

But her love and support for him as a man of integrity never wavered. A letter was found among her papers after her death. We do not know when she sent it, or more probably gave it, to Darwin, but he must have kept it for many years, and put it among his own private papers for her to find again. At the end of it he had written: 'When I am dead, know that many times I have kissed and cried over this. C.D.' As an insight into the effect that Darwin's theories had within his own family, the letter is a most moving and revealing document:

The state of mind that I wish to preserve with respect to you is to feel that while you are acting conscientiously and sincerely wishing and trying to learn the truth, you cannot be wrong, but there are some reasons that force themselves upon me, and prevent myself from being always able to give myself this comfort. I dare say you have often thought of them before, but I will write down what has been in my head, knowing that my own dearest will indulge me.

Your mind and time are full of the most interesting subjects and thoughts of the most absorbing kind, viz. following up your own discoveries – but which make it very difficult for you to avoid casting out as interruptions other sorts of thoughts which have no relation to what you are pursuing, or to be able to give your whole attention to both sides of the question. . . .

It seems to me also that the line of your pursuits may have led you to view chiefly the difficulties on one side, and that you have not had time to consider and study the chain of difficulties on the other; but I believe you do not consider your opinion as formed.

May not the habit in scientific pursuits of believing nothing till it is proved, influence your mind too much in other things which cannot be proved in the same way, and which if true, are likely to be above our comprehension?...

I do not know whether this is arguing as if one side were true and the other false, which I meant to avoid, but I think not. I do not quite agree with you in what you once said that luckily there were no doubts as to how one ought to act. I think prayer is an instance to the contrary, in one case it is a positive duty and perhaps not in the other.

But I dare say you meant in actions which concern others and then I agree with you almost if not quite. I do not wish for any answer to all this – it is a satisfaction to me to write it, and when I talk to you about it I cannot say exactly what I wish to say, and I know you will have patience with your own dear wife. Don't think that it is not my affair and that it does not much signify to me. Everything that concerns you concerns me, and I should be most unhappy if I thought we did not belong to each other forever....

Emma had sensed the profound change in Man's view of his own world which her husband's theories would inevitably bring. But she refused to allow it to affect their life together. Throughout all the public outcry and acrimony, the two people at the centre of the storm held on to their dignity and mutual love. They looked on tempests and were never shaken.

It is ironic but true that Darwin's long delay in publishing *The Origin of Species*, which nearly cost him his place among the giants of scientific discovery, must have been due in large measure to his concern for the religious susceptibilities of his wife.

CHRISTOPHER RALLING

SOURCES

The full texts of Journal, Autobiography and Diary have been published as follows:

1. *Journal of Researches into the Geology and Natural History of the various countries visited during the Voyage of HMS* Beagle *round the World* (first published 1839; new edition by Dent/Everyman 1906, with many reprints. Currently titled *The Voyage of the* Beagle).

2. *The Autobiography of Charles Darwin 1809–1882*, edited by Nora Barlow (Collins 1958).

3. *Charles Darwin's Diary of the Voyage of HMS* Beagle, edited by Nora Barlow (CUP 1933). Selections from the text of the Diary are included in *The Beagle Record* by R. D. Keynes, to appear in 1979 from the same publisher.

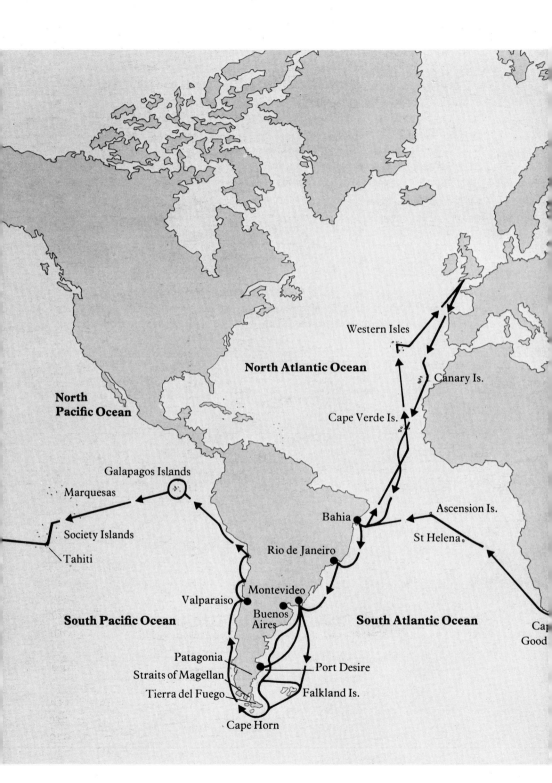

Western Isles

North Atlantic Ocean

North Pacific Ocean

North Pacific Ocean

Canary Is.

Cape Verde Is.

Galapagos Islands

Marquesas

Ascension Is.

Bahia

St Helena

Society Islands

Rio de Janeiro

Tahiti

Valparaiso

Montevideo

South Pacific Ocean

Buenos Aires

South Atlantic Ocean

Cap
Good

Patagonia

Port Desire

Straits of Magellan

Tierra del Fuego

Falkland Is.

Cape Horn

To Cape Verdes, Azores and Falmouth (2 Oct 1836)

Pernambuco

From Devonport (27 Dec 1831)

Bahia

From Ascension Island (see large map)

Callao

Iquique

Rio de Janeiro

Maldonado

Copiapó

Montevideo

Coquimbo

Santa Fé

Valparaiso

Mercédes

Mendoza

Santiago Buenos Aires

Concepción

Valdivia

Bahia Blanca

Carmen

Chilóe

Port Desire

San Julián

Santa Cruz River

Falkland Is.

Tierra del Fuego

South America showing the course of the *Beagle* and Darwin's inland journeys

Indian Ocean

Madagascar

Keeling Is.

Mauritius

Bourbon Is.

Sydney

Bay of Islands

King George's Sound

Tasmania

Hobart

The Voyage of the *Beagle* 1831-6

Thus, from the war of nature, from famine and death, the most exalted object which we are capable of conceiving, namely, the production of the higher animals, directly follows. There is grandeur in this view of life, with its several powers, having been originally breathed by the Creator into a few forms or into one; and that, whilst this planet has gone cycling on according to the fixed law of gravity, from so simple a beginning endless forms most beautiful and most wonderful have been, and are being evolved.

The closing words of *The Origin of Species* by Charles Darwin.

Recollections of the development of my mind and character *from the Autobiography*

I was born at Shrewsbury on 12 February 1809. I have heard my father say that he believed that persons with powerful minds generally had memories extending far back to a very early period of life. This is not my case, for my earliest recollection goes back only to when I was a few months over four years old, when we went to near Abergele for sea-bathing, and I recollect some events and places there with some little distinctness.

My mother died in July 1817, when I was a little over eight years old, and it is odd that I can remember hardly anything about her except her death-bed, her black velvet gown, and her curiously constructed work-table. I believe that my forgetfulness is partly due to my sisters, owing to their great grief, never being able to speak about her or mention her name; and partly to her previous invalid state. In the spring of this same year I was sent to a day school in Shrewsbury, where I stayed a year. Before going to school I was educated by my sister Caroline, but I doubt whether this plan answered. I have been told that I was much slower in learning than my younger sister Catherine, and I believe that I was in many ways a naughty boy. Caroline was extremely kind, clever and zealous; but she was too zealous in trying to improve me; for I clearly remember, after this long interval of years, saying to myself when about to enter a room where she was: 'What will she blame me for now?' – and I made myself dogged, so as not to care what she might say.

By the time I went to this day school my taste for natural history, and more especially for collecting, was well developed. I tried to make out the names of plants, and collected all sorts of things: shells, seals, franks, coins and minerals. The passion for collecting, which leads a man to be a systematic naturalist, a virtuoso or a miser, was very strong in me, and was clearly innate, as none of my sisters or brother ever had this taste.

One little event during this year has fixed itself very firmly in my mind, and I hope that it has done so from my conscience having been afterwards sorely troubled by it; it is curious as showing that apparently I was interested at this early age in the variability of plants! I told another little boy that I could produce variously coloured polyanthuses and primroses by watering them with certain coloured fluids, which was of course a monstrous fable, and had never been tried by me. I may here also confess that as a little boy I was much given to inventing deliberate falsehoods, and this was always done for the sake of causing excitement. For instance, I once gathered much valuable fruit from my father's trees and hid them in the shrubbery, and then ran in breathless haste to spread the news that I had discovered a hoard of stolen fruit. . . .

In the summer of 1818 I went to Dr Butler's great school in Shrewsbury, and remained there for seven years till midsummer 1825, when I was sixteen years old. I boarded at this school, so that I had the great advantage of living the life of a true schoolboy; but, as the distance was hardly more than a mile to my home, I very often ran there in the longer intervals between the callings over and before locking up at night. This I think was in many ways advantageous to me, by keeping up home affections and interests. I remember in the early part of my school life that I often had to run very quickly to be in time, and from being a fleet runner was generally successful. But when in doubt I prayed earnestly to God to help me, and I well remember that I attributed my success to the prayers and not to my quick running, and marvelled how generally I was aided.

I have heard my father and elder sisters say that I had, as a very young boy, a strong taste for long solitary walks; but what I thought about I know not. I often became quite absorbed, and once, whilst returning to school on the summit of the old fortifications round Shrewsbury – which had been converted into a public foot-path with no parapet on one side – I walked off and fell to the ground; but the height was only seven or eight feet. Nevertheless the number of thoughts which passed through my mind during this very short, but sudden and wholly unexpected fall, was astonishing, and seem hardly compatible with what physiologists have, I believe, proved about each thought requiring quite an appreciable amount of time. . . .

I can say in my own favour that I was as a boy humane, but I owed this entirely to the instruction and example of my sisters. I doubt indeed whether humanity is a natural or innate quality. I was very fond of collecting eggs, but I never took more than a single egg out of a bird's nest, except on one single occasion, when I took all, not for their value, but from a sort of bravado.

I had a strong taste for angling, and would sit for any number of hours on the bank of a river or pond watching the float; when at Maer [the Shropshire house of his uncle Josiah Wedgwood] I was told that I could kill the worms with salt and water, and from that day I never spitted a living worm, though at the expense, probably, of some loss of success. . . .

Nothing could have been worse for the development of my mind than Dr Butler's school, as it was strictly classical, nothing else being taught exept a little ancient geography and history. The school as a means of education to me was simply a blank. During my whole life I have been singularly incapable of mastering any language. Especial attention was paid to verse-making, and this I could never do well. I had many friends, and got together a grand collection of old verses, which by patching together, sometimes aided by other boys, I could work into any subject. Much attention was paid to learning by heart the lessons of the previous day; this I could effect with great facility learning forty or fifty lines of Virgil or Homer, whilst I was in morning chapel; but this exercise was utterly useless, for every verse was forgotten in forty-eight hours. I was not idle, and with the exception of versification, generally worked conscientiously at my classics, not using cribs. The sole pleasure I ever received from such studies, was from some of the odes of Horace, which I admired greatly.

When I left the school I was for my age neither high nor low in it; and I believe that I was considered by all my masters and by my father as a very ordinary boy, rather below the common standard in intellect. To my deep mortification my father once said to me, 'You care for nothing but shooting, dogs, and rat-catching, and you will be a disgrace to yourself and all your family.' But my father, who was the kindest man I ever knew, and whose memory I love with all my heart, must have been angry and somewhat unjust when he used such words. . . .

My father was about 6 feet 2 inches in height, with broad shoulders, and very corpulent, so that he was the largest man whom I ever saw. When he last weighed himself, he was 24 stone, but afterwards increased much in weight. His chief mental characteristics were his powers of observation and his sympathy, neither of which have I ever seen exceeded or even equalled. His sympathy was not only with the distresses of others, but in a greater degree with the pleasures of all around him. This led him to be always scheming to give pleasure to others, and, though hating extravagance, to perform many generous actions. . . .

Owing to my father's skill in winning confidence he received many strange confessions of misery and guilt. He often remarked how many miserable wives he had known. In several instances, husbands and wives had gone on pretty well together for between twenty and thirty years, and then hated each other bitterly: this he attributed to their having lost a common bond in their young children having grown up. . . .

My father used to tell me many little things which he had found useful in his medical practice. Thus, ladies often cried much while telling him their troubles, and thus caused much loss of his precious time. He soon found that begging them to command and restrain themselves always made them weep the more, so that afterwards he always encouraged them to go on crying, saying that this would relieve them more than anything else, with the invariable result that they soon ceased to cry, and he could hear what they had to say and give his advice. . . .

In another case my father told a lady that her husband would certainly die. Some months afterwards he saw the widow who was a very sensible woman, and she said, 'You are a very young man, and allow me to advise you always to give, as long as you possibly can, hope to any near relation nursing a patient. You made me despair, and from that moment I lost strength.' My father said that he had often since seen the paramount importance, for the sake of the patient, of keeping up the hope and with it the strength of the nurse in charge. This he sometimes found it difficult to do compatibly with truth. . . .

My father's mind was not scientific, and he did not try to generalise his knowledge under general laws; yet he formed a theory for almost everything which occurred. I do not think that I gained much from him intellectually; but his example ought to have been of much moral service to all his children. One of his golden rules (a hard one to follow) was, 'Never become the friend of any one whom you cannot respect'. . . .

Looking back as well as I can at my character during my school life, the only qualities which at this period promised well for the future, were, that I had strong and diversified tastes, much zeal for whatever interested me, and a keen pleasure in understanding any complex subject or thing. I was taught Euclid by a private tutor, and I distinctly remember the intense satisfaction which the clear geometrical proofs gave me. I remember with equal distinctness the delight which my uncle gave me (the father of Francis Galton) by explaining the principle of the vernier of a barometer. With respect to diversified tastes, independently of science, I was fond of reading various books, and I used to sit for hours reading the historical plays of Shakespeare, generally in an old window in the thick walls of the school. I read also other poetry, such as the recently published poems of Byron, Scott, and Thomson's *Seasons*. I mention this because later in life I wholly lost, to my great regret, all pleasure from poetry of any kind, including Shakespeare. In connection with pleasure from poetry I may add that in 1822 a vivid delight in scenery was first awakened in my mind, during a riding tour on the borders of Wales, and which has lasted longer than any other aesthetic pleasure.

Early in my schooldays a boy had a copy of the *Wonders of the World*, which I often read, and disputed with other boys about the veracity of some of the statements; and I believe this book first gave me a wish to travel in remote countries, which was ultimately fulfilled by the voyage of the *Beagle*. In the latter part of my school life I became passionately fond of shooting, and I do not believe that anyone could have shown more zeal for the most holy cause than I did for shooting birds. How well I remember killing my first snipe, and my excitement was so great that I had much difficulty in reloading my gun from the trembling of my hands. This taste long continued and I became a very good shot. When at Cambridge I used to practise throwing up my gun to my shoulder before a looking-glass to see that I threw it up straight. Another and better plan was to get a friend to wave about a lighted candle, and then to fire at it with a cap on the nipple; and if the aim was accurate, the little puff of air would blow out the candle. The explosion of the cap caused a sharp crack, and I was told that the Tutor of the College remarked, 'What an extraordinary thing it is: Mr Darwin seems to spend hours in cracking a horse-whip in his room, for I often hear the crack when I pass under his windows.'

I had many friends amongst the schoolboys, whom I loved dearly, and I think that my disposition was then very affectionate. Some of these boys were rather clever, but I may add on the principle of 'noscitur a socio' ['by his friends is he known'] that not one of them ever became in the least distinguished.

With respect to science, I continued collecting minerals with much zeal, but quite unscientifically: all that I cared for was a new *named* mineral, and I hardly attempted to classify them. I must have observed insects with some little care, for when at ten years old (1819) I went for three weeks to Plas Edwards [Barmouth] on the sea-coast in Wales, I was very much interested and surprised at seeing a large black and scarlet hemipterous insect, many moths (zygæna) and a cicindela, which are not found in Shropshire. I almost made up my mind to begin collecting all the insects which I could find dead, for on consulting my sister, I concluded that it was not right to kill insects for the sake of making a collection. From reading White's *Selborne* I took much pleasure in watching the habits of birds, and even made notes on the subject. In my simplicity I remember wondering why every gentleman did not become an ornithologist.

Towards the close of my school life, my brother worked hard at chemistry and made a fair laboratory with proper apparatus in the toolhouse in the garden, and I was allowed to aid him as a servant in most of his experiments. He made all the gases and many compounds, and I read with care several books on chemistry, such as Henry and Parkes' *Chemical Catechism*. The subject interested me greatly, and we often used to go on working till rather late at night. This was the best part of my education at school, for it showed me practically the meaning of experimental science. The fact that we worked at chemistry somehow got known at school, and, as it was an unprecedented fact, I was nicknamed 'Gas'. I was also once publicly rebuked by the headmaster, Dr Butler, for thus wasting my time over such useless subjects; and he called me very unjustly a 'poco curante' [lackadaisical], and as I did not understand what he meant it seemed to me a fearful reproach.

As I was doing no good at school, my father wisely took me away at a rather earlier age than usual, and sent me (October 1825) to Edinburgh University with my brother, where I stayed for two years or sessions. My brother was completing his medical studies, though I do not believe he ever really intended to practise, and I was sent there to commence them. But soon after this period I became convinced from various small circumstances that my father would leave me property enough to subsist on with some comfort, though I never imagined that I should be so rich a man as I am; but my belief was sufficient to check any strenuous effort to learn medicine.

The instruction at Edinburgh was altogether by lectures, and these were intolerably dull, with the exception of those on chemistry by Hope; but to my mind there are no advantages and many disadvantages in lectures compared with reading. Dr Duncan's lectures on Materia Medica at eight o'clock on a winter's morning are something fearful to remember. Dr Munro made his lectures on human anatomy as dull as he was himself, and the subject disgusted me. It has proved one of the greatest evils in my life that I was not urged to practise dissection, for I should soon have got over my disgust; and the practice would have been invaluable for all my future work. This has been an irremediable evil, as well as my incapacity to draw. I also attended regularly the clinical wards in the hospital. Some of the cases distressed me a good deal, and I still have vivid pictures before me of some of them; but I was not so foolish as to allow this to lessen my attendance. I cannot understand why this part of my medical course did not interest me in a greater degree; for during the summer before coming to Edinburgh I began attending some of the poor people, chiefly children and women in Shrewsbury: I wrote down as full an account as I could of the cases with all the symptoms, and read them aloud to my father, who suggested further enquiries, and advised me what medicines to give, which I made up myself. At one time I had at least a dozen patients, and I felt a keen interest in the work. My father, who was by far the best judge of character whom I ever knew, declared that I should make a successful physician – meaning by this one who got many patients. He maintained that the chief element of success was exciting confidence; but what he saw in me which convinced him that I should create confidence I know not. I also attended on two occasions the operating theatre in the hospital at Edinburgh, and saw two very bad operations, one on a child, but I rushed away before they were completed. Nor did I ever attend again, for hardly any inducement would have been strong enough to make me do so, this being long before the blessed days of chloroform. The two cases fairly haunted me for many a long year....

During my second year in Edinburgh I attended Jameson's lectures on geology and zoology, but they were incredibly dull. The sole effect they produced on me was the determination never as long as I lived to read a book on geology or in any way to study the science. Yet I feel sure I was prepared for a philosophical treatment of the subject; for an old Mr Cotton in Shropshire who knew a good deal about rocks had pointed out to me two or three years previously a well-known large erratic boulder in the town of Shrewsbury, called the bell-stone. He told me that there was no rock of the same kind nearer than Cumberland or Scotland, and he solemnly assured me that the world would come to an end before anyone would be able to explain how this stone came where it now lay. This produced a deep impression on me and I meditated over this wonderful stone. So that I felt the keenest delight when I first read of the action of icebergs in transporting boulders, and I gloried in the progress of geology....

My summer vacations during these two years were wholly given up to amusements, though I always had some book in hand, which I read with interest. During the summer of 1826, I took a long walking tour with two friends with knapsacks on our backs through North

Wales. We walked thirty miles most days, including one day the ascent of Snowdon. I also went with my sister Caroline on a riding tour in North Wales, a servant with saddle-bags carrying our clothes. The autumns were devoted to shooting, chiefly at Mr Owen's at Woodhouse, and at my Uncle Jos's, at Maer. My zeal was so great that I used to place my shooting boots open by my bedside when I went to bed, so as not to lose half a minute in putting them on in the morning; and on one occasion I reached a distant part of the Maer estate on 20 August for black-game shooting, before I could see: I then toiled on with the gamekeeper the whole day through thick heath and young Scotch firs.

I kept an exact record of every bird which I shot throughout the whole season. One day when shooting at Woodhouse with Captain Owen, the eldest son and Major Hill, his cousin, afterwards Lord Berwick, both of whom I liked very much, I thought myself shamefully used, for every time after I had fired and thought that I had killed a bird, one of the two acted as if loading his gun and cried out, 'You must not count that bird, for I fired at the same time,' and the gamekeeper, perceiving the joke, backed them up. After some hours they told me the joke, but it was no joke to me, for I had shot a large number of birds; but did not know how many, and could not add them to my list, which I used to do by making a knot in a piece of string tied to a button-hole. This my wicked friends had perceived. . . .

My visits to Maer during these two and the three succeeding years were quite delightful, independently of the autumnal shooting. Life there was perfectly free; the country was very pleasant for walking or riding; and in the evening there was much very agreeable conversation, not so personal as it generally is in large family parties, together with music. In the summer the whole family used often to sit on the steps of the old portico, with the flower-garden in front, and with the steep wooded bank, opposite the house, reflected in the lake, with here and there a fish rising or a waterbird paddling about. Nothing has left a more vivid picture on my mind than these evenings at Maer. I was also attached to and greatly revered my Uncle Jos: he was silent and reserved so as to be a rather awful man; but he sometimes talked openly with me. He was the very type of an upright man with the clearest judgment. I do not believe that any power on earth could have made him swerve an inch from what he considered the right course. . . .

After having spent two sessions in Edinburgh, my father perceived, or he heard from my sisters, that I did not like the thought of being a physician, so he proposed that I should become a clergyman. He was very properly vehement against my turning an idle sporting man, which then seemed my probable destination. I asked for some time to consider, as from what little I had heard and thought on the subject I had scruples about declaring my belief in all the dogmas of the Church of England; though otherwise I liked the thought of being a country clergyman. Accordingly I read with care Pearson on the Creed and a few other books on divinity; and as I did not then in the least doubt the strict and literal truth of every word in the Bible, I soon persuaded myself that our creed must be fully accepted. It never struck me how illogical it was to say that I believed in what I could not understand, and what is in fact unintelligible. I might have said with entire truth that I had no wish to dispute any dogma; but I never was such a fool as to feel and say 'credo quia incredibile' ['I believe because it is incredible'].

Considering how fiercely I have been attacked by the orthodox it seems ludicrous that I once intended to be a clergyman. Nor was this intention, and my father's wish, ever formally given up, but died a natural death when, on leaving Cambridge, I joined the *Beagle* as naturalist. If the phrenologists are to be trusted, I was well fitted in one respect to be a clergyman. A few years ago the secretaries of a German psychological society asked me earnestly by letter for a photograph of myself; and some time afterwards I received the proceedings of one of the meetings in which it seemed that the shape of my head had been the subject of a public discussion, and one of the speakers declared that I had the Bump of Reverence developed enough for ten priests.

As it was decided that I should be a clergyman, it was necessary that I should go to one of the English universities and take a degree; but as I had never opened a classical book since leaving school, I found to my dismay that in the two intervening years I had actually forgotten, incredible as it may appear, almost everything which I had learnt even to some few of the Greek letters. I did not therefore proceed to Cambridge at the usual time in October, but worked with a private tutor in Shrewsbury and went to Cambridge after the Christmas vacation, early in 1828. I soon recovered my school standard of knowledge, and could translate easy Greek books, such as Homer and the Greek Testament with moderate facility.

During the three years which I spent at Cambridge my time was wasted, as far as the academical studies were concerned, as completely as at Edinburgh and at school. I attempted mathematics, and even went during the summer of 1828 with a private tutor (a very dull man) to Barmouth; but I got on very slowly. The work was repugnant to me, chiefly from my not being able to see any meaning in the early steps in algebra. This impatience was very foolish, and in after years I have deeply regretted that I did not proceed far enough at least to understand something of the great leading principles of mathematics; for men thus endowed seem to have an extra sense. But I do not believe that I should ever have succeeded beyond a very low grade. With respect to Classics I did nothing except attend a few compulsory college lectures, and the attendance was almost nominal. In my second year I had to work for a month or two to pass the Little Go [entrance examination], which I did easily. Again in my last year I worked with some earnestness for my final degree of BA, and brushed up my classics together with a little algebra and Euclid, which latter gave me much pleasure, as it did whilst at school....

Although, as we shall presently see, there were some redeeming features in my life at Cambridge, my time was sadly wasted there and worse than wasted. From my passion for shooting and for hunting and when this failed for riding across country, I got into a sporting set, including some dissipated low-minded young men. We used often to dine together in the evening, though these dinners often included men of a higher stamp, and we sometimes drank too much, with jolly singing and playing at cards afterwards. I know that I ought to feel ashamed of days and evenings thus spent, but, as some of my friends were very pleasant and we were all in the highest spirits, I cannot help looking back to these times with much pleasure.

But I am glad to think that I had many other friends of a widely different nature. I was very intimate with Whitley, who was afterwards Senior Wrangler [top mathematician of his year], and we used continually to take long walks together. He inoculated me with a taste for pictures and good engravings, of which I bought some. I frequently went to the Fitzwilliam Gallery, and my taste must have been fairly good, for I certainly admired the best pictures, which I discussed with the old curator....

I also got into a musical set, I believe by means of my warm-hearted friend Herbert, who took a high wrangler's degree. From associating with these men and hearing them play I acquired a strong taste for music, and used very often to time my walks so as to hear on weekdays the anthem in King's College Chapel. This gave me intense pleasure, so that my backbone would sometimes shiver. I am sure that there was no affectation or mere imitation in this taste, for I used generally to go by myself to King's College, and

I sometimes hired the chorister boys to sing in my rooms. Nevertheless I am so utterly destitute of an ear, that I cannot perceive a discord, or keep time and hum a tune correctly; and it is a mystery how I could possibly have derived pleasure from music.

My musical friends soon perceived my state, and sometimes amused themselves by making me pass an examination, which consisted in ascertaining how many tunes I could recognise, when they were played rather more quickly or slowly than usual. 'God save the King' when thus played was a sore puzzle. There was another man with almost as bad an ear as I had, and strange to say he played a little on the flute. Once I had the triumph of beating him in one of our musical examinations.

But no pursuit at Cambridge was followed with nearly so much eagerness or gave me so much pleasure as collecting beetles. It was the mere passion for collecting, for I did not dissect them and rarely compared their external characters with published descriptions, but got them named anyhow. I will give a proof of my zeal: one day, on tearing off some old bark, I saw two rare beetles and seized one in each hand; then I saw a third and new kind, which I could not bear to lose, so that I popped the one which I held in my right hand into my mouth. Alas, it ejected some intensely acrid fluid, which burnt my tongue so that I was forced to spit the beetle out, which was lost, as well as the third one.

I was very successful in collecting and invented two new methods; I employed a labourer to scrape, during the winter, moss off old trees and place [it] in a large bag, and likewise to collect the rubbish at the bottom of the barges in which reeds are brought from the fens; and thus I got some very rare species. No poet ever felt more delight at seeing his first poem published than I did at seeing in Stephen's *Illustrations of British Insects* the magic words, 'captured by C. Darwin, Esq.' It seems therefore that a taste for collecting beetles is some indication of future success in life! ...

I have not as yet mentioned a circumstance which influenced my whole career more than any other. This was my friendship with Prof. Henslow. Before coming up to Cambridge, I had heard of him from my brother as a man who knew every branch of science, and I was accordingly prepared to reverence him. He kept open house once every week, where all undergraduates and several older members of the University, who were attached to science, used to meet in the evening. I soon got, through [W.D.] Fox [Darwin's cousin], an invitation, and went there regularly. Before long I became well acquainted with Henslow, and during the latter half of my time at Cambridge took long walks with him on most days; so that I was called by some of the dons 'the man who walks with Henslow'; and in the evening I was very often asked to join his family dinner. His knowledge was great in botany, entomology, chemistry, mineralogy and geology. His strongest taste was to draw conclusions from long-continued minute observations. His judgment was excellent, and his whole mind well-balanced; but I do not suppose that anyone would say that he possessed much original genius. . . .

Henslow's benevolence was unbounded, as he proved by his many excellent schemes for his poor parishioners, when in after years he held the living of Hitcham. My intimacy with such a man ought to have been and I hope was an inestimable benefit. . . .

Looking back, I infer that there must have been something in me a little superior to the common run of youths, otherwise the above-mentioned men, so much older than me and higher in academical position, would never have allowed me to associate with them. Certainly I was not aware of any such superiority, and I remember one of my sporting friends, Turner, who saw me at work on my beetles, saying that I should some day be a Fellow of the Royal Society, and the notion seemed to me preposterous.

During my last year at Cambridge I read with care and profound interest Humboldt's *Personal Narrative*. This work and Sir J. Herschel's *Introduction to the Study of Natural Philosophy* stirred up in me a burning zeal to add even the most humble contribution to the noble structure of Natural Science. No one or a dozen other books influenced me nearly so much as these two. . . .

My summer vacations were given up to collecting beetles, to some reading and short tours. In the autumn my whole time was devoted to shooting, chiefly at Woodhouse and Maer. . . . Upon the whole the three years which I spent at Cambridge were the most joyful in my happy life; for I was then in excellent health, and almost always in high spirits.

As I had at first come up to Cambridge at Christmas, I was forced to keep two terms after passing my final examination, at the commencement of 1831; and Henslow then persuaded me to begin the study of geology. Therefore on my return to Shropshire I examined sections and coloured a map of parts round Shrewsbury. Professor Sedgwick intended to visit North Wales in the beginning of August to pursue his famous geological investigation amongst the older rocks, and Henslow asked him to allow me to accompany him. Accordingly he came and slept at my Father's house.

A short conversation with him during this evening produced a strong impression on my mind. Whilst examining an old gravel-pit near Shrewsbury, a labourer told me that he had found in it a large, worn tropical Volute shell, such as may be seen on the chimney-pieces of cottages; and as he would not sell the shell I was convinced that he had really found it in the pit. I told Sedgwick of the fact, and he at once said (no doubt truly) that it must have been thrown away by someone into the pit; but then added, if really embedded there it would be the greatest misfortune to geology, as it would overthrow all that we know about the superficial deposits of the midland counties. These gravel-beds belonged in fact to the glacial period, and in after years I found in them broken arctic shells. But I was then utterly astonished at Sedgwick not being delighted at so wonderful a fact as a tropical shell being found near the surface in the middle of England. Nothing before had ever made me thoroughly realise, though I had read various scientific books, that science consists in grouping facts so that general laws or conclusions may be drawn from them.

Next morning we started for Llangollen, Conway, Bangor and Capel Curig. This tour was of decided use in teaching me a little how to make out the geology of a country. Sedgwick often sent me on a line parallel to his, telling me to bring back specimens of the rocks and to mark the stratification on a map. I have little doubt that he did this for my good, as I was too ignorant to have aided him. On this tour I had a striking instance how easy it is to overlook phenomena, however conspicuous, before they have been observed by anyone. We spent many hours in Cwm Idwal, examining all the rocks with extreme care, as Sedgwick was anxious to find fossils in them. But neither of us saw a trace of the wonderful glacial phenomena all around us; we did not notice the plainly scored rocks, the perched boulders, the lateral and terminal moraines. Yet these phenomena are so conspicuous that, as I declared in a paper published many years afterwards in the *Philosophical Magazine*, a house burnt down by fire did not tell its story more plainly than did this valley. If it had still been filled by a glacier, the phenomena would have been less distinct than they now are.

At Capel Curig I left Sedgwick and went in a straight line by compass and map across the mountains to Barmouth, never following any track unless it coincided with my course. I thus came on some strange wild places and enjoyed much this manner of travelling. I visited Barmouth to see some Cambridge friends who were reading there, and thence returned to Shrewsbury and to Maer for shooting; for at that time I should have thought myself mad to give up the first days of partridge-shooting for geology or any other science.

On returning home from my short geological tour in North Wales, I found a letter from Henslow, informing me that Captain FitzRoy was willing to give up part of his own cabin to any young man who would volunteer to go with him without pay as naturalist to the voyage of the *Beagle*. . . . I was instantly eager to accept the offer, but my father strongly objected, adding the words fortunate for me, 'If you can find any man of common sense, who advises you to go, I will give my consent'. So I wrote that evening and refused the offer. On the next morning I went to Maer to be ready for 1 September, and whilst out shooting, my uncle sent for me, offering to drive me over to Shrewsbury and talk with my father. As my uncle thought it would be wise in me to accept the offer, and as my father always maintained that he was one of the most sensible men in the world, he at once consented in the kindest manner. I had been rather extravagant at Cambridge and to console my father said, 'that I should be deuced clever to spend more than my allowance whilst on board the *Beagle*'; but he answered with a smile, 'But they all tell me you are very clever.'

Next day I started for Cambridge to see Henslow, and thence to London to see FitzRoy, and all was soon arranged. Afterwards on becoming very intimate with FitzRoy, I heard that I had run a very narrow risk of being rejected, on account of the shape of my nose! He was an ardent disciple of Lavater, and was convinced that he could judge a man's character by the outline of his features; and he doubted whether anyone with my nose could possess sufficient energy and determination for the voyage. But I think he was afterwards well-satisfied that my nose had spoken falsely.

FitzRoy's character was a singular one, with many very noble features: he was devoted to his duty, generous to a fault, bold, determined, indomitably energetic, and an ardent friend to all under his sway. He would undertake any sort of trouble to assist those whom he thought deserved assistance. He was a handsome man, strikingly like a gentleman, with highly courteous manners, which resembled those of his maternal uncle, the famous Lord Castlereagh, as I was told by the Minister at Rio. Nevertheless he must have inherited much in his appearance from Charles II, for Dr Wallich gave me a collection of photographs which he had made, and I was struck with the resemblance of one to FitzRoy; on looking at the name, I found it Ch. E. Sobieski Stuart, Count d'Albanie, illegitimate descendent of the same monarch. . . .

On 11 September [1831] I paid a flying visit with FitzRoy to the

Sketch of Darwin c. 1838, possibly by Richmond

Beagle at Plymouth. Thence to Shrewsbury, to wish my father and sisters a long farewell. On 24 October, I took up my residence at Plymouth, and remained there until 27 December, when the *Beagle* finally left the shores of England for her circumnavigation of the world. We made two earlier attempts to sail, but were driven back each time by heavy gales. These two months at Plymouth were the most miserable which I ever spent, though I exerted myself in various ways. I was out of spirits at the thought of leaving all my family and friends for so long a time, and the weather seemed to me inexpressibly gloomy. I was also troubled with palpitations and pain about the heart, and like many a young ignorant man, especially one with a smattering of medical knowledge, was convinced that I had heart-disease. I did not consult any doctor, as I fully expected to hear the verdict that I was not fit for the voyage, and I was resolved to go at all hazards....

Setting Sail

DIARY 23 NOVEMBER 1831

This has been a very important day in the annals of the Beagle; at one o'clock she was loosed from the moorings and sailed about a mile to Barnett pool. Here she will remain till the day of sailing arrives. This little sail was to me very interesting, everything so new and different to what one has ever seen: the Coxswain's piping, the manning the yards, the men working at the hawsers to the sound of a fife; but nothing is so striking as the rapidity and decision of the orders, and the alertness with which they are obeyed. There remains very little to be done to make all ready for sailing. All the stores are completed and yesterday between five and six thousand canisters of preserved meat were stowed away. Not one inch of room is lost; the hold would contain scarcely another bag of bread. My notions of the inside of a ship were about as indefinite as those of some men on the inside of a man, viz. a large cavity containing air, water and food, mingled in hopeless confusion....

4 DECEMBER

I am writing this for the first time on board. It is now about one o'clock, and I intend sleeping in my hammock, I did so last night and experienced a most ludicrous difficulty in getting into it: my great fault of jockeyship was in trying to put my legs in first. The hammock being suspended, I thus only succeeded in pushing [it] away without making any progress in inserting my own body. The correct method is to sit accurately in centre of bed, then give yourself a dexterous twist, and your head and feet come into their respective places. After a little time I daresay I shall, like others, find it very comfortable. I have spent the day partly on board and partly with my brother: in the evening, Captain King and son, Stokes [assistant surveyor], my brother and myself dined with Captain FitzRoy.

In the morning the ship rolled a good deal, but I did not feel uncomfortable. This gives me great hopes of escaping seasickness. I find others trust in the same weak support. May we not be confounded....

An idle day. Dined for the first time in Captain's cabin and felt quite at home. Of all the luxuries the Captain has given me, none will be so essential as that of having my meals with him. I am often afraid I shall be quite overwhelmed with the number of subjects which I ought to take into hand. It is difficult to mark out any plan and without method on shipboard, I am sure little will be done. The principal objects are, first, collecting, observing and reading in all branches of Natural History that I possibly can manage. Observations in Meteorology, French and Spanish, Mathematics and a little Classics, perhaps not more than Greek Testament on Sundays. I hope generally to have some one English book in hand for my amusement, exclusive of the above mentioned branches. If I have not energy enough to make myself steadily industrious during the voyage, how great and uncommon an opportunity of improving myself shall I throw away. May this never for one moment escape my mind, and then perhaps I may have the same opportunity of drilling my mind that I threw away whilst at Cambridge.

14 DECEMBER

A beautiful day, giving great hopes of a fair wind. Took my usual and delightful walk in the beautiful country around Mount Edgcombe. Everything connected with dressing and sleeping have hitherto been my greatest drawbacks to comfort, but even these difficulties are wearing away. My hammock, after endless alterations, has been made flat, and I have trained myself to a regular method in dressing and undressing.

Orders are issued for sailing tomorrow morning....

26 DECEMBER

A beautiful day, and an excellent one for sailing: the opportunity has been lost owing to the drunkenness and absence of nearly the whole crew. The ship has been all day in state of anarchy. One day's holiday has caused all this mischief; such a scene proves how absolutely necessary strict discipline is amongst such thoughtless beings as sailors. Several have paid the penalty for insolence, by sitting for eight or nine hours in heavy chains. Whilst in this state, their conduct was like children, abusing every body and thing but themselves, and the next moment nearly crying. It is an unfortunate beginning, being obliged so early to punish so many of our best men; there was however no choice left as to the necessity of doing it. Dined in gun-room and had a pleasant evening.

After having been twice driven back by heavy south-western gales, Her Majesty's ship *Beagle*, a ten-gun brig, under the command of Captain FitzRoy, RN, sailed from Devonport on 27 December 1831. The object of the expedition was to complete the survey of Patagonia and Tierra del Fuego, commenced under Captain King in 1826 to 1830; to survey the shores of Chile, Peru, and of some islands in the Pacific; and to carry a chain of chronometrical measurements round the world.

DIARY 28 DECEMBER

Waked in the morning with an eight-knot-per-hour wind, and soon became sick, and remained so during the whole day. My thoughts most unpleasantly occupied with the flogging of several men for offences brought on by the indulgence granted them on Christmas Day. I am doubtful whether this makes their crime [of] drunkenness and consequent insolence more or less excusable.

29 DECEMBER

At noon we were 380 miles from Plymouth, the remaining distance to Madeira being 800 miles. We are in the Bay of Biscay, and there is a good deal of swell on the sea. I have felt a good deal [of] nausea several times in the day. There is one great difference between my former seasickness and the present: absence of giddiness. Using my eyes is not unpleasant: indeed it is rather amusing whilst lying in my hammock to watch the moon or stars performing their small revolutions in their new apparent orbits. I will now give all the dear-bought experience I have gained about seasickness.

In first place the misery is excessive, and far exceeds what a person would suppose who had never been at sea more than a few days. I found the only relief to be in a horizontal position: but that it must never be forgotten the more you combat with the enemy the sooner will he yield. I found the only thing my stomach would bear was biscuit and raisins: but of this, as I became more exhausted, I soon grew tired, and then the sovereign remedy is sago, with wine and spice, and made very hot. But the only sure thing is lying down, and if in a hammock so much the better.

The evenings already are perceptibly longer and weather much milder.

30 DECEMBER

At noon lat. 43 South of Cape Finisterre and across the famous Bay of Biscay: wretchedly out of spirits and very sick. I often said before starting that I had no doubt I should frequently repent of the whole undertaking. Little did I think with what fervour I should do so. I can scarcely conceive any more miserable state than when such dark and gloomy thoughts are haunting the mind as have today pursued me. I staggered for a few minutes on deck, and was much struck by the appearance of the sea. The deep water differs as much from that near shore as an inland lake does from a little pool. It is not only the darkness of the blue, but the brilliancy of its tint when contrasted with the white curling tip, that gives such a novel beauty to the scene. I have seen paintings that give a faithful idea of it....

6 JANUARY 1832

After heaving to during the night we came in sight of Tenerife at day break, bearing south-west about twelve miles off. We are now a few miles, tacking with a light wind to Santa Cruz, which at this distance looks a small town, built of white houses and lying very flat. Point Naga, which we are doubling, is a rugged, uninhabited mass of lofty rock with a most remarkably bold and varied outline. In drawing it you could not make a line straight. Every thing has a beautiful appearance: the colours are so rich and soft. The peak, or sugarloaf, has just shown itself above the clouds. It towers in the sky twice as high as I should have dreamed of looking for it. A dense bank of clouds entirely separates the snowy top from its rugged base. It is now about 11 o'clock and I must have another gaze at this long-wished-for object of my ambition.

Oh misery, misery: we were just preparing to drop our anchor within half a mile of Santa Cruz, when a boat came alongside, bringing with it our death-warrant. The consul declared we must perform a rigorous quarantine of twelve days. Those who have never experienced it can scarcely conceive what a gloom it cast on every one: matters were soon decided by the Captain ordering all sail to be set and make a course for the Cape Verde Islands. And we have left perhaps one of the most interesting places in the world, just at the moment when we were near enough for every object to create, without satisfying, our utmost curiosity. The abrupt valleys which divided in parallel rows the brown and desolate hills were spotted with patches of a light green vegetation, and gave the scenery to me a very novel appearance. I suppose, however, that volcanic islands under the same zone have much the same character.

Generally the atmosphere is hazy; and this is caused by the falling of impalpably fine dust, which was found to have slightly injured the astronomical instruments. The morning before we anchored at Porto Praya, I collected a little packet of this brown-coloured fine dust, which appeared to have been filtered from the wind by the gauze of the vane at the mast-head. Mr Lyell has also given me four packets of dust which fell on a vessel a few hundred miles northward of these islands. Professor Ehrenberg finds that this dust consists in great part of infusoria with siliceous shields, and of the siliceous tissue of plants. In five little packets which I sent him, he has ascertained no less than sixty-seven different organic forms! The infusoria, with the exception of two marine species, are all inhabitants of fresh water. I have found no less than fifteen different accounts of dust having fallen on vessels when far out in the Atlantic. From the direction of the wind whenever it has fallen, and from its having always fallen during those months when the harmattan [a dry land-wind of Upper Guinea, which blows from December to February] is known to raise clouds of dust high into the atmosphere, we may feel sure that it all comes from Africa. It is, however, a very singular fact, that, although Professor Ehrenberg knows many species of infusoria peculiar to Africa, he finds none of these in the dust which I sent him: on the other hand, he finds in it two species which hitherto he knows as living only in South America. The dust falls in such quantities as to dirty everything on board, and to hurt people's eyes; vessels even have run on shore owing to the obscurity of the atmosphere. It has often fallen on ships when several hundred, and even more than a thousand miles from the coast of Africa, and at points 1600 miles distant in a north and south direction. In some dust which was collected on a vessel 300 miles from the land, I was much surprised to find particles of stone above the thousandth of an inch square, mixed with finer matter. After this fact one need not be surprised at the diffusion of the far lighter and smaller sporules of cryptogamic plants.

DIARY 13 FEBRUARY

This has been the first day that the heat has annoyed us, and in proportion all have enjoyed the delicious coolness of the moonlight evenings: but when in bed, it is I am sure like what one would feel if stewed in very warm melted butter. This morning a glorious fresh trade wind is driving us along. I call it glorious because others do: it is, however, bitter cruelty to call anything glorious that gives my stomach so much uneasiness. Oh, a ship is a true pandemonium, and the cawkers who are hammering away above my head veritable devils. . . .

Saw the rocks of St Paul's right ahead: heaved to during the night, and this morning we were a few miles distant from them. When within three miles, two boats were lowered, one with Mr Stokes for surveying the island, the other with Mr Wickham and myself for geologising and shooting. St Paul's may be considered as the top of a submarine mountain. It is not above forty feet above the sea, and about half a mile in circumference. Bottom could not be found within a mile of the island, and if the depth of the Atlantic is as great as it is usually supposed, what an enormous pyramid this must be.

We had some difficulty in landing, as the long swell of the open sea broke with violence on the rocky coast. We had seen from a distance large flocks of sea-birds soaring about, and when we were on the island a most extraordinary scene was presented. We were surrounded on every side by birds, so unaccustomed to men that they would not move. We knocked down with stones and my hammer the active and swift tern. Shooting was out of the question, so we got two of the boat's crew and the work of slaughter commenced. They soon collected a pile of birds, and hats full of eggs.

Whilst we were so active on shore, the men in the boat were not less so. They caught a great number of fine large fish and would have succeeded much better, had not the sharks broken so many of their hooks and lines. They contrived to land three of these latter fish, and during our absence two large ones were caught from the ship. We returned in great triumph with our prey, but were a good deal fatigued. The island is only fifty miles from the equator, and the rocks, being white from the birds' dung, reflected a glaring heat. The birds were only of two sorts, booby and noddies, and these, with a few insects, were the only organised beings that inhabited this desolate spot.

In the evening the ceremonies for crossing the line commenced. The officer on watch reported a boat ahead. The Captain turned 'hands up, shorten sail', and we heaved to in order to converse with Mr Neptune. The Captain held a conversation with him through a speaking trumpet, the result of which was that he would in the morning pay us a visit.

17 FEBRUARY

We have crossed the Equator, and I have undergone the disagreeable operation of being shaved. About nine o'clock this morning we poor 'griffins', two and thirty in number, were put all together on the lower deck. The hatchways were battened down, so we were in the dark and very hot. Presently, four of Neptune's constables came to us and one by one led us up on deck. I was the first and escaped easily: I nevertheless found this watery ordeal sufficiently disagreeable. Before coming up, the constable blindfolded me and, thus led along, buckets of water were thundered all around. I was then placed on a plank, which could be easily tilted up into a large bath of water. They then lathered my face and mouth with pitch and paint, and scraped some of it off with a piece of roughened iron hoop: a signal being given, I was tilted head over heels into the water, where two men received me and ducked me. At last, glad enough, I escaped: most of the others were treated much worse, dirty mixtures being put in their mouths and rubbed on their faces. The whole ship was a shower-bath, and water was flying about in every direction. Of course not one person, even the Captain, got clear of being wet through. . . .

25 FEBRUARY
Since leaving Tenerife the sea has been so calm that it is hard to believe it the same element which tossed us about in the Bay of Biscay. This stillness is of great moment to the quantity of comfort which is attainable on ship-board. Hitherto I have been surprised how enjoyable life is in this floating prison. But the greatest and most constant drawback to this is the very long period which separates us from our return. Excepting when in the midst of tropical scenery, my greatest share of pleasure is in anticipating a future time when I shall be able to look back on past events; and the consciousness that this prospect is so distant never fails to be painful. To enjoy the soft and delicious evenings of the tropics, to gaze at the bright band of stars, which stretches from Orion to the Southern Cross, and to enjoy such pleasures in quiet solitude, leaves an impression which a few years will not destroy.

26 FEBRUARY
For the first time in my life I saw the sun at noon to the north: yesterday it was very near over our heads and therefore of course we are a little to the south of it. I am constantly surprised at not finding the heat more intense than it is. When at sea and with a gentle breeze blowing one does not even wish for colder weather. I am sure I have frequently been more oppressed by a hot summer's day in England.

27 FEBRUARY
Quietly sailing. Tomorrow we shall reach Bahia.

Brazil

DIARY 29 FEBRUARY

The day has passed delightfully: delight is, however, a weak term for such transports of pleasure: I have been wandering by myself in a Brazilian forest. Amongst the multitude it is hard to say what set of objects is most striking; the general luxuriance of the vegetation bears the victory, the elegance of the grasses, the novelty of the para-sitical plants, the beauty of the flowers, the glossy green of the foliage, all tend to this end. A most paradoxical mixture of sound and silence pervades the shady parts of the wood....

1 MARCH

I can only add raptures to the former raptures. I walked with the two mids. a few miles into the interior. The country is composed of small hills, and each new valley is more beautiful than the last. I collected a great number of brilliantly-coloured flowers, enough to make a florist go wild. Brazilian scenery is nothing more nor less than a view in the Arabian Nights, with the advantage of reality. The air is deliciously cool and soft; full of enjoyment, one fervently desires to live in retirement in this new and grander world....

4 MARCH

This day is the first of the Carnival, but Wickham, Sullivan and myself, nothing daunted, were determined to face its dangers. These dangers consist in being unmercifully pelted by wax balls full of water, and being wet through by large tin squirts. We found it very difficult to maintain our diginity whilst walking through the streets. Charles V has said that he was a brave man who could snuff a candle with his fingers without flinching: I say it is he who can walk at a steady pace when buckets of water on each side are ready to be dashed over him. After an hour's walking the gauntlet, we at length reached the country and there we were well determined to remain till it was dark. We did so, and had some difficulty in finding the road back again, as we took care to coast along the outside of the town. To complete our ludicrous miseries, a heavy shower wet us to the skins; and at last gladly we reached the *Beagle*. It was the first time Wickham had been on shore and he vowed if he was here for six months it should be [the] only one.

5 MARCH

King and myself started at nine o'clock for a long naturalising walk. Some of the valleys were even more beautiful than any I have yet seen. There is a wild luxuriance in these spots that is quite enchanting. One of the great superiorities that tropical scenery has over European is the wildness even of the cultivated ground. Coconuts, bananas, plantain, oranges, papaws are mingled as if by Nature, and between them are patches of the herbaceous plants such as Indian corn, yams and cassada [cassava]: and in this class of views, the knowledge that all conduces to the subsistence of mankind, adds much to the pleasure of beholding them. We returned to the ship about half after five o'clock, and during these eight hours we scarcely rested one. The sky was cloudless and the day very hot, yet we did not suffer much. It appears to me that the heat merely brings on indolence, and if there is any motive sufficient to overcome this, it is very easy to undergo a good deal of fatigue. During the walk I was chiefly employed in collecting numberless small beetles and in geologising. King shot some pretty birds and I a most beautiful large lizard. It is a new and pleasant thing for me to be conscious that naturalising is doing my duty, and that if I neglected that duty I should at [the] same time neglect what has for some years given me so much pleasure....

15 MARCH

Everybody is delighted with the excellent manners of the negroes. I gave my friends at the vênda [inn] some wine, and when I parted with them it is my firm belief, no duchess with three tails could have given such court-like and dignified bows as the black women saluted me with.

JOURNAL I was amused by watching the habits of the Diodon antennatus, which was caught swimming near the shore. This fish, with its flabby skin, is well known to possess the singular power of distending itself into a nearly spherical form. After having been taken out of the water for a short time, and then again immersed in it, a considerable quantity both of water and air is absorbed by the mouth, and perhaps likewise by the branchial orifices....

This diodon possessed several means of defence. It could give a severe bite, and could eject water from its mouth to some distance, at the same time making a curious noise by the movement of its jaws. By the inflation of its body, the papillæ with which the skin is covered become erect and pointed. But the most curious circumstance is, that it secretes from the skin of its belly, when handled, a most beautiful carmine-red fibrous matter which stains ivory and paper in so permanent a manner, that the tint is retained with all its brightness to the present day; I am quite ignorant of the nature and use of this secretion. I have heard from Dr Allan of Forres, that he had frequently found a diodon, floating alive and distended, in the stomach of the shark; and that on several occasions he has known it eat its way, not only through the coats of the stomach, but through the sides of the monster, which has thus been killed. Who would ever have imagined that a little soft fish could have destroyed the great and savage shark?

DIARY 18 MARCH

Against a strong tide we slowly stood out of the bay of All Saints and took a lasting farewell of Bahia. If I have already seen enough of the tropics to be allowed to judge, my report would be most favourable; nothing can be more delightful than the climate, and in beauty the sky and landscape are unparalleled in a colder zone.

RIO DE JANEIRO, 3–8 APRIL 1832

DIARY 3 APRIL

All day we ran along the coast and in the evening drew near to the harbour of Rio. The whole line is irregularly mountainous, and interspersed with hills of singular forms. The opening of the port is recognised by one of these, the well-known Sugarloaf. As it would be impossible to get a good anchorage or enjoy the view so late in the evening, the captain has put the ship's head to the wind and we shall, to my great joy, cruise about for the night. We have seen great quantities of shipping; and what is quite as interesting, porpoises, sharks and turtles. Altogether, it has been the most idle day I have spent since I left England. Everybody is full of anxiety about letters and newspapers. Tomorrow morning our fates will be decided.

JOURNAL 5 APRIL

A few days after our arrival I became acquainted with an Englishman [named Patrick Lennon] who was going to visit his estate, situated rather more than a hundred miles from the capital, to the northward of Cape Frio. I gladly accepted his kind offer of allowing me to accompany him.

DIARY 6 APRIL

The day has been frittered away in obtaining the passports for my expedition into the interior. It is never very pleasant to submit to the insolence of men in office, but to the Brazilians, who are as contemptible in their minds as their persons are miserable, it is nearly intolerable. But the prospect of wild forests tenanted by beautiful birds, monkeys and sloths, and lakes by cavies and alligators, will make any naturalist lick the dust even from the foot of a Brazilian.

JOURNEY TO MACAÉ ESTATE, 8–23 APRIL 1832

JOURNAL 8 APRIL

Our party amounted to seven. The first stage was very interesting. The day was powerfully hot, and as we passed through the woods, everything was motionless, excepting the large and brilliant butterflies, which lazily fluttered about. The view seen when crossing the hills behind Praia Grande was most beautiful: the colours were intense, and the prevailing tint a dark blue; the sky and the calm waters of the bay vied with each other in splendour. After passing through some cultivated country, we entered a forest, which in the grandeur of all its parts could not be exceeded. We arrived by midday at Ithacaia. This small village is situated on a plain, and round the central house are the huts of the negroes. These, from their regular form and position, reminded me of the drawings of the Hottentot habitations in Southern Africa. As the moon rose early, we determined to start the same evening for our sleeping-place at the Lagoa Marica. As it was growing dark we passed under one of the massive, bare and steep hills of granite which are so common in this country.

This spot is notorious from having been, for a long time, the residence of some runaway slaves, who, by cultivating a little ground near the top, contrived to eke out a subsistence. At length they were discovered, and a party of soldiers being sent, the whole were seized, with the exception of one old woman, who, sooner than again be led into slavery, dashed herself to pieces from the summit of the mountain. In a Roman matron this would have been called the noble love of freedom: in a poor negress it is mere brutal obstinacy.

We continued riding for some hours. For the few last miles the road was intricate, and it passed through a desert waste of marshes and lagoons. The scene by the dimmed light of the moon was most desolate. A few fireflies flitted by us; and the solitary snipe, as it rose, uttered its plaintive cry. The distant and sullen roar of the sea scarcely broke the stillness of the night.

9 APRIL

We left our miserable sleeping-place before sunrise. The road passed through a narrow sandy plain, lying between the sea and the interior salt lagoons. The number of beautiful fishing birds, such as egrets and cranes, and the succulent plants assuming most fantastical forms, gave to the scene an interest which it would not otherwise have possessed. The few stunted trees were loaded with parasitical plants, among which the beauty and delicious fragrance of some of the orchidæ were most to be admired. As the sun rose, the day became extremely hot, and the reflection of the light and heat from the white sand was very distressing. We dined at Mandetiba, the thermometer in the shade being 84°. The perfectly calm water of an extensive lagoon, quite refreshed us. As the vênda here was a very good one, and I have the pleasant, but rare remembrance, of an excellent dinner, I will be grateful and presently describe it, as the type of its class.

These houses are often large, and are built of thick upright posts, with boughs interwoven, and afterwards plastered. They seldom have floors, and never glazed windows; but are generally pretty well roofed. Universally the front part is open, forming a kind of verandah, in which tables and benches are placed. The bedrooms join on each side, and here the passenger may sleep as comfortably as he can, on a wooden platform, covered by a thin straw mat. The vênda stands in a courtyard, where the horses are fed. On first arriving, it was our custom to unsaddle the horses and give them their Indian corn; then, with a low bow, to ask the senhór to do us the favour to give us something to eat. 'Anything you choose, sir,' was his usual answer. For the few first times, vainly I thanked providence for having guided us to so good a man. The conversation proceeding, the case universally became deplorable. 'Any fish can you do us the favour of giving?' – 'Oh! no, sir.' 'Any soup?' – 'No, sir.' 'Any bread?' – 'Oh! no, sir.' 'Any dried meat?' – 'Oh! no, sir.'

If we were lucky, by waiting a couple of hours, we obtained fowls, rice, and farinha [meal]. It not unfrequently happened that we were obliged to kill, with stones, the poultry for our own supper. When, thoroughly exhausted by fatigue and hunger, we timorously hinted that we should be glad of our meal, the pompous, and (though true) most unsatisfactory answer was, 'It will be ready when it is ready'. If we had dared to remonstrate any further, we should have been told to proceed on our journey, as being too impertinent. The hosts are most ungracious and disagreeable in their manners; their houses and their persons are often filthily dirty; the want of the accommodation of forks, knives, and spoons is common; and I am sure no cottage or hovel in England could be found in a state so utterly destitute of every comfort. . . .

14 APRIL

Leaving Socêgo, we rode to another estate on the Rio Macaé, which was the last patch of cultivated ground in that direction. The estate was two and a half miles long, and the owner had forgotten how many broad. Only a small piece had been cleared, yet almost every acre was capable of yielding all the various rich productions of a tropical land. Considering the enormous area of Brazil, the proportion of cultivated ground can scarcely be considered as anything, compared to that which is left in the state of nature: at some future age, how vast a population it will support! During the second day's journey we found the road so shut up that it was necessary that a man should go ahead with a sword to cut away the creepers.

The forest abounded with beautiful objects; among which the tree ferns, though not large, were, from their bright green foliage and the elegant curvature of their fronds, most worthy of admiration. In the evening it rained very heavily, and although the thermometer stood at 65°, I felt very cold. As soon as the rain ceased, it was curious to observe the extraordinary evaporation which commenced over the whole extent of the forest. At the height of a hundred feet the hills were buried in a dense white vapour, which rose like columns of smoke from the most thickly-wooded parts, and especially from the valleys. I observed this phenomenon on several occasions: I suppose it is owing to the large surface of foliage, previously heated by the sun's rays.

While staying at this estate, I was very nearly being an eye-witness to one of those atrocious acts which can only take place in a slave country. Owing to a quarrel and a lawsuit, the owner was on the point of taking all the women and children from the male slaves, and selling them separately at the public auction at Rio. Interest, and not any feeling of compassion, prevented this act. Indeed, I do not believe the inhumanity of separating thirty families, who had lived together for many years, even occurred to the owner. Yet I will pledge myself that, in humanity and good feeling, he was superior to the common run of men. It may be said there exists no limit to the blindness of interest and selfish habit.

I may mention one very trifling anecdote, which at the time struck me more forcibly than any story of cruelty. I was crossing a ferry with a negro, who was uncommonly stupid. In endeavouring to make him understand, I talked loud, and made signs, in doing which I passed my hand near his face. He, I suppose, thought I was in a passion, and was going to strike him; for instantly, with a frightened look and half-shut eyes, he dropped his hands. I shall never forget my feelings of surprise, disgust, and shame, at seeing a great powerful man afraid even to ward off a blow, directed, as he thought, at his face. This man had been trained to a degradation lower than the slavery of the most helpless animal....

18 APRIL

In returning we spent two days at Socêgo, and I employed them in collecting insects in the forest.... Many of the older trees presented a very curious appearance from the tresses of a liana hanging from their boughs, and resembling bundles of hay. If the eye was turned from the world of foliage above to the ground beneath, it was attracted by the extreme elegance of the leaves of the ferns and mimosæ. The latter in some parts, covered the surface with a brush-wood only a few inches high. In walking across these thick beds of mimosæ, a broad track was marked by the change of shade, produced by the drooping of their sensitive petioles. It is easy to specify the individual objects of admiration in these grand scenes; but it is not possible to give an adequate idea of the higher feelings of wonder, astonishment and devotion, which fill and elevate the mind.

19–23 APRIL

Leaving Socêgo, during the two first days we retraced our steps. It was very wearisome work, as the road generally ran across a glaring-hot, sandy plain, not far from the coast. I noticed that each time the horse put its foot on the fine siliceous sand, a gentle chirping noise was produced. On the third day we took a different line, and passed through the gay little village of Madre de Dios. This is one of the principal lines of road in Brazil; yet it was in so bad a state that no wheel[ed] vehicle, excepting the clumsy bullock-wagon, could pass along. In our whole journey we did not cross a single bridge built of stone; and those made of logs of wood were frequently so much out of repair that it was necessary to go on one side to avoid them. All distances are inaccurately known. The road is often marked by crosses, in the place of milestones, to signify where human blood has been spilled. On the evening of the 23rd we arrived at Rio, having finished our pleasant little excursion.

During the remainder of my stay at Rio, I resided in a cottage at Botofogo Bay. It was impossible to wish for anything more delightful than thus to spend some weeks in so magnificent a country. In England any person fond of natural history enjoys in his walks a great advantage, by always having something to attract his attention; but in these fertile climates, teeming with life, the attractions are so numerous, that he is scarcely able to walk at all....

Every one has heard of the beauty of the scenery near Botofogo. The house in which I lived was seated close beneath the well-known mountain of the Corcovado. It has been remarked, with much truth, that abruptly conical hills are characteristic of the formation which Humboldt designates as gneiss-granite. Nothing can be more striking than the effect of these huge rounded masses of naked rock rising out of the most luxuriant vegetation.

I was often interested by watching the clouds, which, rolling in from seaward, formed a bank just beneath the highest point of the Corcovado. This mountain, like most others, when thus partly veiled, appeared to rise to a far prouder elevation than its real height of 2300 feet. Mr Daniell has observed, in his meteorological essays, that a cloud sometimes appears fixed on a mountain summit, while the wind continues to blow over it. The same phenomenon here presented a slightly different appearance. In this case the cloud was clearly seen to curl over, and rapidly pass by the summit, and yet was neither diminished nor increased in size. The sun was setting, and a gentle southerly breeze, striking against the southern side of the rock, mingled its current with the colder air above; and the vapour was thus condensed. But as the light wreaths of cloud passed over the ridge and came within the influence of the warmer atmosphere of the northern sloping bank, they were immediately redissolved....

Nature, in these climes, chooses her vocalists from more humble performers than in Europe. A small frog, of the genus Hyla, sits on a blade of grass about an inch above the surface of the water, and sends forth a pleasing chirp: when several are together they sing in harmony on different notes. I had some difficulty in catching a specimen of this frog. The genus Hyla has its toes terminated by small suckers; and I found this animal could crawl up a pane of glass, when placed absolutely perpendicular. Various cicadæ and crickets, at the same time, keep up a ceaseless shrill cry, but which, softened by the distance, is not unpleasant. Every evening after dark this great concert commenced; and often have I sat listening to it, until my attention has been drawn away by some curious passing insect.... Sitting down on a block of granite, it was delightful to watch the various insects and birds as they flew past. The humming-bird seems particularly fond of such shady retired spots. Whenever I saw these little creatures buzzing round a flower, with their wings vibrating so rapidly as to be scarcely visible, I was reminded of the sphinx moths: their movements and habits are indeed in many respects very similar.

Following a pathway I entered a noble forest, and from a height of five or six hundred feet one of those splendid views was presented, which are so common on every side of Rio. At this elevation the landscape attains its most brilliant tint; and every form, every shade, so completely surpasses in magnificence all that the European has ever beheld in his own country, that he knows not how to express his feelings. The general effect frequently recalled to my mind the gayest scenery of the opera house or the great theatres.

I never returned from these excursions empty-handed. This day I found a specimen of a curious fungus, called Hymenophallus. Most people know the English Phallus, which in autumn taints the air with its odious smell: this, however, as the entomologist is aware, is to some of our beetles a delightful fragrance. So was it here; for a Strongylus, attracted by the odour, alighted on the fungus as I carried it in my hand. We here see in two distant countries a similar relation between plants and insects of the same families, though the species of both are different. When man is the agent in introducing into a country a new species, this relation is often broken: as one instance of this I may mention, that the leaves of the cabbages and lettuces, which in England afford food to such a multitude of slugs and caterpillars, in the gardens near Rio are untouched.

During our stay at Brazil I made a large collection of insects. A few general observations on the comparative importance of the different orders may be interesting to the English entomologist. The large and brilliantly-coloured Lepidoptera bespeak the zone they inhabit far more plainly than any other race of animals. I allude only to the butterflies, for the moths, contrary to what might have been expected from the rankness of the vegetation, certainly appeared in much fewer numbers than in our own temperate regions. I was much surprised at the habits of Papilio feronia. This butterfly is not uncommon, and generally frequents the orange-groves. Although a

Brazilian scenery is nothing more nor less than a view in the Arabian Nights, with the advantage of reality. (p. 40)

. . . The beauty and delicious fragrance of some of the orchidae were most to be admired. (p. 44)

MILTONIA SPECTABILIS VAR. MORELIANA

MILTONIA CLOWESII

SOPHRONITIS CERNUA

I collected a number of brilliantly-coloured flowers, enough to make a florist go wild.   (p. 40)

HELICONIA COLLINSIANA

COUROUPITA

SOLANUM

WILD CALLIANDRA

HERRANIA SP.

PHALLUS INDUSIATUS

... *I found a specimen of a curious fungus*
(left), *called Hymenophallus.*   (p. 48)

The large and brilliantly-coloured Lepidoptera bespeak the zone they inhabit far more plainly than any other race of animals. (p. 48)

PHOEBIS AND ASCIA BUTTERFLIES

AGRAULIS VANILLAE

HELICONIUS MELPOMENE

EPIPHYLE OREA

RHETUS PERIANDER

PHYCIODES LANDSDORFI

DIAETHRIA MERIDIONALIS

PREPONA LAERTES

The number of minute and obscurely-coloured beetles is exceedingly great. . . . It is sufficient to disturb the composure of an entomologist's mind, to look forward to the future dimensions of the complete catalogue.

(P. 57)

ENTIMUS FORMOSUS VIANA

TRACHYDERES STRIATUS

UNIA GRACILLOR

CURCULIONID BEETLE

TAUROMA CASTA

STRATEGUS ALOEUS

CASSID BEETLE

CHRYSOMELID BEETLE

CASSID BEETLE

Papilio feronia, ... although a high flier, ... frequently alights on the trunks of trees. On these occasions its head is invariably placed downwards, and its wings expanded in a horizontal plane. (p. 48)

(Left) *Whenever I saw* [humming-birds] *buzzing round a flower, with their wings vibrating so rapidly as to be scarcely visible, I was reminded of the sphinx moths: their movements and habits are indeed in many respects very similar.* (p. 48)

FLORISUGA MELLIVORA

(Above) *An army of never-failing foragers may be seen, some going forth, and others returning, burdened with pieces of green leaf, often larger than their own bodies.* (p. 57)

(Left) *A small frog, of the genus Hyla, sits on a blade of grass about an inch above the surface of the water, and sends forth a pleasing chirp.* (p. 47)

HYLA PULCHELLA

high flier, yet it very frequently alights on the trunks of trees. On these occasions its head is invariably placed downwards; and its wings are expanded in a horizontal plane, instead of being folded vertically, as is commonly the case. This is the only butterfly which I have ever seen that uses its legs for running. Not being aware of this fact, the insect, more than once, as I cautiously approached with my forceps, shuffled on one side just as the instrument was on the point of closing, and thus escaped. But a far more singular fact is the power which this species possesses of making a noise. Several times when a pair, probably male and female, were chasing each other in an irregular course, they passed with[in] a few yards of me; and I distinctly heard a clicking noise, similar to that produced by a toothed wheel passing under a spring catch. The noise was continued at short intervals, and could be distinguished at about twenty yards' distance: I am certain there is no error in the observation.

I was disappointed in the general aspect of the Coleoptera. The number of minute and obscurely-coloured beetles is exceedingly great. The cabinets of Europe can, as yet, boast only of the larger species from tropical climates. It is sufficient to disturb the composure of an entomologist's mind, to look forward to the future dimensions of a complete catalogue....

A person, on first entering a tropical forest, is astonished at the labour of the ants: well-beaten paths branch off in every direction, on which an army of never-failing foragers may be seen, some going forth, and others returning, burdened with pieces of green leaf, often larger than their own bodies.

A small dark-coloured ant sometimes migrates in countless numbers. One day, at Bahia, my attention was drawn by observing many spiders, cockroaches and other insects, and some lizards, rushing in the greatest agitation across a bare piece of ground. A little way behind, every stalk and leaf was blackened by a small ant. The swarm having crossed the bare space, divided itself, and descended an old wall. By this means many insects were fairly enclosed; and the efforts which the poor little creatures made to extricate themselves from such a death were wonderful. When the ants came to the road they changed their course, and in narrow files reascended the wall. Having placed a small stone so as to intercept one of the lines, the whole body attacked it, and then immediately retired. Shortly afterwards another body came to the charge, and again having failed to make any impression, this line of march was entirely given up. By going an inch round, the file might have avoided the stone, and this doubtless would have happened, if it had been originally there: but having been attacked, the lion-hearted little warriors scorned the idea of yielding....

I was much interested one day by watching a deadly contest between a pepsis and a large spider of the genus Lycosa. The wasp made a sudden dash at its prey, and then flew away: the spider was evidently wounded, for, trying to escape, it rolled down a little slope, but had still strength sufficient to crawl into a thick tuft of grass. The wasp soon returned, and seemed surprised at not immediately finding its victim. It then commenced as regular a hunt as ever hound did after fox; making short semicircular casts, and all the time rapidly vibrating its wings and antennæ. The spider, though well concealed, was soon discovered; and the wasp, evidently still afraid of its adversary's jaws, after much manœuvring, inflicted two stings on the under side of its thorax. At last, carefully examining with its antennæ the now motionless spider, it proceeded to drag away the body. But I stopped both tyrant and prey.

[*While the* Beagle *sailed northwards to survey the coast, Darwin remained in the cottage at Botofogo, where he continued this programme of naturalising and geologising, hunting and exploring. When the* Beagle *got back, it was learned that a party which had gone up-river from Rio had all caught fever, from which three had died. They set sail again on 5 July southwards to Monte-video.*]

In the morning we got under way, and stood out of the splendid harbour of Rio de Janeiro. In our passage to the Plata, we saw nothing particular, excepting on one day a great shoal of porpoises, many hundreds in number. The whole sea was in places furrowed by them; and a most extraordinary spectacle was presented, as hundreds, proceeding together by jumps in which their whole bodies were exposed, thus cut the water. When the ship was running nine knots an hour, these animals could cross and recross the bows with the greatest ease, and then dash away right ahead.

As soon as we entered the estuary of the Plata, the weather was very unsettled. One dark night we were surrounded by numerous seals and penguins, which made such strange noises that the officer on watch reported he could hear the cattle bellowing on shore. On a second night we witnessed a splendid scene of natural fireworks: the masthead and yard-arm-ends shone with St Elmo's light, and the form of the vane could almost be traced, as if it had been rubbed with phosphorus. The sea was so highly luminous that the tracks of the penguins were marked by a fiery wake, and the darkness of the sky was momentarily illuminated by the most vivid lightning.

When within the mouth of the river, I was interested by observing how slowly the waters of the sea and river mixed. The latter, muddy and discoloured, from its less specific gravity, floated on the surface of the salt water. This was curiously exhibited in the wake of the vessel, where a line of blue water was seen mingling in little eddies, with the adjoining fluid.

MONTEVIDEO, 26 JULY TO 19 AUGUST 1832

DIARY 26 JULY
We entered the bay about nine o'clock. Just as we were coming to an anchor, signals were made from the *Druid*, a frigate lying here; which (to our utter astonishment and amusement) ordered us to 'Clear for action' and shortly after 'Prepare to cover our boats'. We set sail. The latter part of the order was shortly explained by the arriving of six boats heavily armed with carronades and containing about forty marines, all ready for fighting, and more than 100 blue jackets. Captain Hamilton came on board and informed us that the present government is a military usurpation; that the head of the party had seized upon 400 horses, the property of a British subject; and that in short the flotilla of boats went to give weight to his arguments.

The revolutions in these countries are quite laughable; some few years ago in Buenos Aires, they had fourteen revolutions in twelve months. Things go as quietly as possible: both parties dislike the sight of blood, so that the one which appears the strongest gains the day. The disturbances do not much affect the inhabitants of the town, for both parties find it best to protect private property. The present governor has about 260 gaucho cavalry and the same number of negro infantry; the opposite party is now collecting a force and the moment he enters the town the others will scamper out. Mr Parry (a leading merchant here) says he is quite certain 150 men from the frigate could any night take Montevideo. The dispute has terminated by a promise of restitution of the horses; but which I do not think is very clear will be kept. I am afraid it is not impossible that the consequences will be very unpleasant to us. The *Druid*'s officers have not for some weeks been allowed to go on shore, and perhaps we shall be obliged to act in the same manner. How annoying will be the sight of green turf plains, whilst we are performing a sort of quarantine on board. . . .

We certainly are a most unquiet ship: peace flies before our steps. On entering the outer roadstead, we passed a Buenos Aires guard-ship. When abreast of her, she fired an empty gun. We, not understanding this, sailed on, and in a few minutes another discharge was accompanied by the whistling of a shot over our rigging. Before she could get another gun ready we had passed her range. When we arrived at our anchorage, which is more than three miles distant from the landing place, two boats were lowered, and a large party started in order to stay some days in the city. Wickham went with us, and intended immediately going to Mr Fox, the English minister, to inform him of the insult offered to the British flag. When close to the shore, we were met by a quarantine boat, which said we must all return on board, to have our bill of health inspected, from fears of the cholera. . . .

During our absence, a boat had come with an officer, whom the Captain soon despatched with a message to his Commander to say, 'He was sorry he was not aware he was entering an uncivilised port, or he would have had his broadside ready for answering his shot.' When our boats and the health one came alongside, the Captain immediately gave orders to get under weigh and return to Montevideo; at the same time, sending to the Governor, through the Spanish officer, the same messages which he had sent to the guard-ship, adding that the case should be thoroughly investigated in other quarters. We then loaded and pointed all the guns on one broadside, and ran down close along the guard-ship: hailed her, and said, that when we again entered the port we would be prepared as at present and if she dared to fire a shot we would send our whole broadside into her rotten hulk. . . .

5 AUGUST

This has been an eventful day in the history of the *Beagle*. At ten o'clock in the morning the minister for the present military government came on board and begged for assistance against a serious insurrection of some black troops. Captain FitzRoy immediately went ashore to ascertain whether it was a party affair, or that the inhabitants were really in danger of having their houses ransacked. The head of the police (Dumas) has continued in power through both governments, and is considered as entirely neutral. Being applied to, he gave it as his opinion that it would be doing a service to the state to land our force. Whilst this was going on ashore, the Americans landed their boats and occupied the Custom House. Immediately the Captain arrived at the mole, he made us the signal to hoist out and man our boats. In a very few minutes, the yawl, cutter, whaleboat and gig were ready with fifty-two men, heavily armed with muskets, cutlasses and pistols. After waiting some time on the pier, Signor Dumas arrived and we marched to a central fort, the seat of government. During this time the insurgents had planted artillery to command some of the streets, but otherwise remained quiet. They had previously broken open the prison and armed the prisoners. The chief cause of apprehension was owing to their being in possession of the citadel, which contains all the ammunition.

It is suspected that all this disturbance is owing to the manœuvring of the former constitutional government. But the politics of the place are quite unintelligible. It has always been said that the interest of the soldiers and the present government are identical; and now it would seem to be the reverse. Captain FitzRoy would have nothing to do with all this: he would only remain to see that private property was not attacked. If the national band were not rank cowards, they might at once seize the citadel and finish the business. Instead of this, they prefer protecting themselves in the fortress of St Lucia. Whilst the different parties were trying to negotiate matters, we remained at our station and amused ourselves by cooking beefsteaks in the courtyard. At sunset the boats were sent on board and one returned with warm clothing for the men to bivouac during the night. As I had a bad headache, I also came and remained on board. The few left in the ship, under the command of Mr Chaffers, have been the most busily engaged of the whole crew. They have triced up the boarding netting, loaded and pointed the guns, and cleared for action. We are now at night in a high state of preparation so as to make the best defence possible, if the *Beagle* should be attacked. To obtain ammunition could be the only possible motive.

6 AUGUST

The boats have returned. Affairs in the city now more decidedly show a party spirit, and as the black troops are enclosed in the citadel by double the number of armed citizens, Captain FitzRoy deemed it advisable to withdraw his force. It is probable in a very short time the two adverse sides will come to an encounter; under such circumstances, Captain FitzRoy, being in possession of the central fort, would have found it very difficult to have preserved his character of neutrality. There certainly is a great deal of pleasure in the excitement of this sort of work; quite sufficient to explain the reckless gaiety with which sailors undertake even the most hazardous attacks. Yet

DIARY as time flies, it is an evil to waste so much in empty parade.

JOURNAL The neighbourhood of the Rio Plata seems peculiarly subject to electric phenomena. In the year 1793, one of the most destructive thunderstorms perhaps on record happened at Buenos Aires: thirty-seven places within the city were struck by lightning, and nineteen people killed. From the facts stated in several books of travels, I am inclined to suspect that thunderstorms are very common near the mouths of great rivers. Is it not possible that the mixture of large bodies of fresh and salt water may disturb the electrical equilibrium? Even during our occasional visits to this part of South America, we heard of a ship, two churches and a house having been struck.

DIARY 22 SEPTEMBER

Had a very pleasant cruise about the bay with the Captain and Sulivan. We stayed some time on Punta Alta, about ten miles from the ship; here I found some rocks. These are the first I have seen, and are very interesting, from containing numerous shells and the bones of large animals. The day was perfectly calm; the smooth water and the sky were indistinctly separated by the ribbon of mudbanks: the whole formed a most unpicturesque picture. It is a pity such bright clear weather should be wasted on a country where half its charms do not appear. We got on board just in time to escape a heavy squall and rain.

24 OCTOBER

The night was pitch-dark, with a fresh breeze. The sea from its extreme luminousness presented a wonderful and most beautiful appearance: every part of the water which by day is seen as foam, glowed with a pale light. The vessel drove before her bows two billows of liquid phosphorus, and in her wake was a milky train. As far as the eye reached the crest of every wave was bright, and from the reflected light the sky just above the horizon was not so utterly dark as the rest of the Heavens. It was impossible to behold this plain of matter, as it were melted and consuming by heat, without being reminded of Milton's description of the regions of Chaos and Anarchy.

[*On leaving Punta Alta, the* Beagle *sailed south to Tierra del Fuego and the Falkland Islands, before returning north to the mouth of the Rio Negro by way of Maldonado in July 1833. In his Journal Darwin grouped together the visits to Tierra del Fuego and placed them at the point where the second (8–10 June 1834) occurs. Darwin's order of events is followed here.*]

Argentina

The *Beagle* sailed from Maldonado, and on 3 August she arrived off the mouth of the Rio Negro. This is the principal river on the whole line of coasts between the Strait of Magellan and the Plata. It enters the sea about 300 miles south of the estuary of the Plata. About fifty years ago, under the old Spanish government, a small colony was established here; and it is still the most southern position (lat. 41°) on this eastern coast of America, inhabited by civilised man.

The country near the mouth of the river is wretched in the extreme: on the south side a long line of perpendicular cliffs commences, which exposes a section of the geological nature of the country. The strata are of sandstone, and one layer was remarkable from being composed of a firmly-cemented conglomerate of pumice pebbles, which must have travelled more than 400 miles, from the Andes. The surface is everywhere covered up by a thick bed of gravel, which extends far and wide over the open plain. Water is extremely scarce, and, where found, is almost invariably brackish. The vegetation is scanty; and although there are bushes of many kinds, all are armed with formidable thorns, which seem to warn the stranger not to enter on these inhospitable regions....

One day I rode to a large salt-lake, or Salina, which is distant fifteen miles from the town.... The border of the lake is formed of mud: and in this numerous large crystals of gypsum, some of which are three inches long, lie embedded; whilst on the surface others of sulphate of soda lie scattered about. The Gauchos call the former the 'padre del sal', and the latter the 'madre'; they state that these progenitive salts always occur on the borders of the salinas, when the water begins to evaporate. The mud is black, and has a fetid odour. I could not at first imagine the cause of this, but I afterwards perceived that the froth which the wind drifted on shore was coloured green, as if by confervæ: I attempted to carry home some of this green matter, but from an accident failed. Parts of the lake seen from a short distance appeared of a reddish colour, and this perhaps was owing to some infusorial animalcula. The mud in many places was thrown up by numbers of some kind of worm, or annelidous animal. How surprising it is that any creature should be able to exist in brine, and that they should be crawling among crystals of sulphate of soda and lime! And what becomes of these worms when, during the long summer, the surface is hardened into a solid layer of salt? Flamingos in considerable numbers inhabit this lake, and breed here; throughout Patagonia, in Northern Chile, and at the Galapagos Islands, I met with these birds wherever there were lakes of brine. I saw them here wading about in search of food – probably for the worms which burrow in the mud; and these latter probably feed on infusoria or confervæ. Thus we have a little living world within itself, adapted to these inland lakes of brine....

As the *Beagle* intended to call at Bahía Blanca, I determined to proceed there by land; and ultimately I extended my plan to travel the whole way by the postas [small military communications-posts] to Buenos Aires.

LAND JOURNEY FROM PATAGONES (MOUTH OF THE RIO NEGRO) TO BAHÍA BLANCA, 11–17 AUGUST 1833

II AUGUST

Mr Harris, an Englishman residing at Patagones, a guide, and five gauchos, who were proceeding to the army on business, were my companions on the journey....

Shortly after passing the first spring we came in sight of a famous tree, which the Indians reverence as the altar of Walleechu. It is situated on a high part of the plain, and hence is a landmark visible at a great distance. As soon as a tribe of Indians come in sight of it, they offer their adorations by loud shouts. The tree itself is low, much branched, and thorny: just above the root it has a diameter of about three feet. It stands by itself without any neighbour, and was indeed the first tree we saw; afterwards we met with a few others of the same kind, but they were far from common. Being winter, the tree had no leaves, but in their place numberless threads, by which the various offerings, such as cigars, bread, meat, pieces of cloth etc had been suspended. Poor Indians, not having anything better, only pull a thread out of their ponchos, and fasten it to the tree. Richer Indians are accustomed to pour spirits and maté [an infusion of leaves of the maté shrub] into a certain hole, and likewise to smoke upwards, thinking thus to afford all possible gratification to Walleechu. To complete the scene, the tree was surrounded by the bleached bones of horses which had been slaughtered as sacrifices....

About two leagues beyond this curious tree we halted for the night: at this instant an unfortunate cow was spied by the lynx-eyed gauchos, who set off in full chase, and in a few minutes dragged her in with their lazos, and slaughtered her. We here had the four necessaries of life 'en el campo' – pasture for the horses, water (only a muddy puddle), meat and firewood. The gauchos were in high spirits at finding all these luxuries; and we soon set to work at the poor cow. This was the first night which I passed under the open sky, with the gear of the recado [South American saddle] for my bed. There is high enjoyment in the independence of the gaucho life: to be able at any moment to pull up your horse, and say, 'Here we will pass the night.' The death-like stillness of the plain, the dogs keeping watch, the gipsy-group of gauchos making their beds round the fire, have left in my mind a strongly-marked picture of this first night, which will never be forgotten.

The next day the country continued similar to that above described. It is inhabited by few birds or animals of any kind. Occasionally a deer, or a guanaco (wild llama) may be seen; but the agouti (Cavia patagonica) is the commonest quadruped. This animal here represents our hares. It differs, however, from that genus in many essential respects: for instance, it has only three toes behind. It is also nearly twice the size, weighing from twenty to twenty-five pounds. The agouti is a true friend of the desert, it is a common feature in the landscape to see two or three hopping quickly one after the other in a straight line across these wild plains. . . .

It is a singular fact that although the agouti is not now found as far south as Port St Julian, yet that Captain Wood, in his voyage in 1670, talks of them as being numerous there. What cause can have altered, in a wide, uninhabited and rarely-visited country, the range of an animal like this? It appears also from the number shot by Captain Wood in one day at Port Desire, that they must have been considerably more abundant there formerly than at present. Where the bizcacha lives and makes its burrows, the agouti uses them; but where, as at Bahía Blanca, the bizcacha is not found, the agouti burrows for itself. The same thing occurs with the little owl of the pampas (Athene cunicularia), which has so often been described as standing like a sentinel at the mouth of the burrows; for in Banda Oriental, owing to the absence of the bizcacha, it is obliged to hollow out its own habitation. . . .

To the northward of the Rio Negro, between it and the inhabited country near Buenos Aires, the Spaniards have only one small settlement, recently established at Bahía Blanca. The distance in a straight line to Buenos Aires is very nearly five hundred British miles. The wandering tribes of horse Indians, which have always occupied the

greater part of this country, having of late much harassed the out-
lying estancias, the government at Buenos Aires equipped some time
since an army under the command of General Rosas for the purpose
of exterminating them. The troops were now encamped on the banks
of the Colorado; a river lying about eighty miles northward of the
Rio Negro. . . .

The next morning, as we approached the Rio Colorado, the
appearance of the country changed. We soon came on a plain
covered with turf, which, from its flowers, tall clover, and little owls,
resembled the Pampas. . . .

The encampment of General Rosas was close to the river. It consisted of a square formed by wagons, artillery, straw huts etc. The
soldiers were nearly all cavalry; and I should think such a villainous,
banditti-like army was never before collected together. The greater
number of men were of a mixed breed, between Negro, Indian and
Spaniard. I know not the reason, but men of such origin seldom have
a good expression of countenance. I called on the Secretary to show
my passport. He began to cross-question me in the most dignified
and mysterious manner. By good luck I had a letter of recommenda-
tion from the government of Buenos Aires to the Commandant of
Patagones. This was taken to General Rosas, who sent me a very
obliging message; and the Secretary returned all smiles and gracious-
ness. We took up our residence in the rancho, or hovel, of a curious
old Spaniard, who had served with Napoleon in the expedition
against Russia.

We stayed two days at the Colorado; I had little to do, for the
surrounding country was a swamp, which in summer (December),
when the snow melts on the Cordillera, is overflowed by the river.
My chief amusement was watching the Indian families as they came
to buy little articles at the rancho where we stayed. It was supposed
that General Rosas had about 600 Indian allies. The men were a
tall, fine race, yet it was afterwards easy to see in the Fuegian savage
the same countenance rendered hideous by cold, want of food and
less civilisation.

Some authors, in defining the primary races of mankind, have
separated these Indians into two classes, but this is certainly incorrect.
Among the young women, or chinas, some deserve to be called even
beautiful. Their hair was coarse, but bright and black; and they wore
it in two plaits hanging down to the waist. They had a high colour,
and eyes that glistened with brilliancy; their legs, feet and arms were
small and elegantly formed; their ankles, and sometimes their waists,
were ornamented by broad bracelets of blue beads. Nothing could

be more interesting than some of the family groups. A mother with one or two daughters would often come to our rancho, mounted on the same horse. They ride like men, but with their knees tucked up much higher. This habit, perhaps, arises from their being accustomed, when travelling, to ride the loaded horses. The duty of the women is to load and unload the horses; to make the tents for the night; in short to be, like the wives of all savages, useful slaves. The men fight, hunt, take care of the horses, and make the riding gear.

One of their chief indoor occupations is to knock two stones together till they become round in order to make the bolas. With this important weapon the Indian catches his game, and also his horse, which roams free over the plain. In fighting, his first attempt is to throw down the horse of his adversary with the bolas, and when entangled by the fall to kill him with the chuzo [the gaucho spear]. If the balls only catch the neck or body of an animal, they are often carried away and lost. As the making the stones round is the labour of two days, the manufacture of the balls is a very common employment. Several of the men and women had their faces painted red, but I never saw the horizontal bands which are so common among the Fuegians. Their chief pride consists in having everything made of silver; I have seen a cacique [chief] with his spurs, stirrups, handle of his knife, and bridle made of this metal: the head-stall and reins being of wire, were not thicker than whipcord; and to see a fiery steed wheeling about under the command of so light a chain, gave to the horsemanship a remarkable character of elegance.

General Rosas intimated a wish to see me, a circumstance which I was afterwards very glad of. He is a man of extraordinary character, and has a most predominant influence in the country, which it seems probable he will use to its prosperity and advancement. He is said to be the owner of seventy-four square leagues of land, and to have about 300,000 head of cattle. His estates are admirably managed, and are far more productive of corn than those of others. He first gained his celebrity by his laws for his own estancias, and by disciplining several hundred men so as to resist with success the attacks of the Indians. There are many stories current about the rigid manner in which his laws were enforced.

One of these was, that no man, on penalty of being put into stocks, should carry his knife on a Sunday. This being the principal day for gambling and drinking, many quarrels arose, which from the general manner of fighting with the knife often proved fatal. One Sunday the Governor came in great form to pay the estancia a visit, and General Rosas, in his hurry, walked out to receive him with his knife, as usual, stuck in his belt. The steward touched his arm, and reminded him of the law; upon which turning to the Governor, he said he was extremely sorry, but that he must go into the stocks, and that till let out, he possessed no power even in his own house. After a little time the steward was persuaded to open the stocks, and to let him out, but no sooner was this done, than he turned to the steward and said, 'You now have broken the laws, so you must take my place in the stocks'. Such actions as these delighted the gauchos, who all possess high notions of their own equality and dignity.

General Rosas is also a perfect horseman – an accomplishment of no small consequence in a country where an assembled army elected its general by the following trial: a troop of unbroken horses being driven into a corral, were let out through a gateway, above which was a crossbar. It was agreed whoever should drop from the bar on one of these wild animals, as it rushed out, and should be able, without saddle or bridle, not only to ride it, but also to bring it back to the door of the corral, should be their general. The person who succeeded was accordingly elected; and doubtless made a fit general for such an army. This extraordinary feat has also been performed by Rosas.

By these means, and by conforming to the dress and habits of the gauchos, he has obtained an unbounded popularity in the country, and in consequence a despotic power. I was assured by an English merchant, that a man who had murdered another, when arrested and questioned concerning his motive, answered, 'He spoke disrespectfully of General Rosas, so I killed him'. At the end of a week the murderer was at liberty. This doubtless was the act of the general's party and not of the general himself.

In conversation he is enthusiastic, sensible and very grave. His gravity is carried to a high pitch: I heard one of his mad buffoons (for he keeps two, like the barons of old) relate the following anecdote: 'I wanted very much to hear a certain piece of music, so I went to the general two or three times to ask him. He said to me, "Go about your business, for I am engaged." I went a second time; he said, "If you come again I will punish you." A third time I asked, and he laughed. I rushed out of the tent, but it was too late; he ordered two soldiers to catch and stake me. I begged by all the saints in heaven he would let me off, but it would not do. When the general laughs he spares neither madman nor sound.' The poor flighty gentleman looked quite dolorous, at the very recollection of the staking. This is a very severe punishment. Four posts are driven into the ground, and the man is extended by his arms and legs horizontally, and there left to stretch for several hours. The idea is evidently taken from the usual method of drying hides. My interview passed away without a smile, and I obtained a passport and order for the government posthorses, and this he gave me in the most obliging and ready manner.

In the morning we started for Bahía Blanca, which we reached in two days. . . .

Bahía Blanca scarcely deserves the name of a village. A few houses and the barracks for the troops are enclosed by a deep ditch and fortified wall. The settlement is only of recent standing (since 1828); and its growth has been one of trouble. The government of Buenos Aires unjustly occupied it by force, instead of following the wise example of the Spanish Viceroys, who purchased the land near the older settlement of the Rio Negro, from the Indians. . . .

22 AUGUST

We passed the night in Punta Alta, and I employed myself in searching for fossil bones, this point being a perfect catacomb for monsters of extinct races. The evening was perfectly calm and clear; the extreme monotony of the view gave it an interest even in the midst of mud-banks and gulls, sand-hillocks and solitary vultures. In riding back in the morning we came across a very fresh track of a puma, but did not succeed in finding it. We saw also a couple of zorillos, or skunks – odious animals, which are far from uncommon.

SURVEYING THE COAST NEAR BAHÍA BLANCA, 24 AUGUST
TO 6 OCTOBER 1833

JOURNAL The *Beagle* arrived [at Bahía Blanca] on 24 August, and a week afterwards sailed for the Plata. With Captain Fitzroy's consent I was left behind, to travel by land to Buenos Aires. I will here add some observations, which were made during this visit and on a previous occasion, when the *Beagle* was employed in surveying the harbour.

The plain, at the distance of a few miles from the coast, belongs to the great Pampean formation, which consists in part of a reddish clay, and in part of a highly calcareous, marly rock. Nearer the coast there are some plains formed from the wreck of the upper plain, and from mud, gravel and sand thrown up by the sea during the slow elevation of the land, of which elevation we have evidence in upraised beds of recent shells, and in rounded pebbles of pumice scattered over the country. At Punta Alta we have a section of one of these later-formed little plains, which is highly interesting from the number and extraordinary character of the remains of gigantic land-animals embedded in it.... I will here give only a brief outline of their nature.

First, parts of three heads and other bones of the Megatherium, the huge dimensions of which are expressed by its name. Secondly, the Megalonyx, a great allied animal. Thirdly, the Scelidotherium, also an allied animal, of which I obtained a nearly perfect skeleton. It must have been as large as a rhinoceros: in the structure of its head it comes, according to Mr Owen [see p. 166], nearest to the Cape Anteater, but in some other respects it approaches to the armadilloes. Fourthly, the Mylodon Darwinii, a closely related genus of little inferior size. Fifthly, another gigantic edental quadruped. Sixthly, a large animal, with an osseous coat in compartments, very like that of an armadillo. Seventhly, an extinct kind of horse.... Eighthly, a tooth of a Pachydermatous animal, probably the same with the Macrauchenia, a huge beast with a long neck like a camel.... Lastly, the Toxodon, perhaps one of the strangest animals ever discovered: in size it equalled an elephant or megatherium, but the structure of its teeth, as Mr Owen states, proves indisputably that it was intimately related to the gnawers, the order which, at the present day, includes most of the smallest quadrupeds: in many details it is allied to the pachydermata: judging from the position of its eyes, ears, and nostrils, it was probably aquatic, like the dugong and manatee, to which it is also allied. How wonderfully are the different orders, at the present time so well separated, blended together in different points of the structure of the Toxodon!

The remains of these nine great quadrupeds and many detached bones were found embedded on the beach, within the space of about 200 yards square. It is a remarkable circumstance that so many different species should be found together; and it proves how numerous in kind the ancient inhabitants of this country must have been....

The remains at Punta Alta were embedded in stratified gravel and reddish mud, just such as the sea might now wash up on a shallow bank. They were associated with twenty-three species of shells, of which thirteen are recent and four others very closely related to recent forms; whether the remaining ones are extinct or simply unknown, must be doubtful, as few collections of shells have been made on this coast. As, however, the recent species were embedded in nearly the same proportional numbers with those now living in the bay, I think there can be little doubt, that this accumulation belongs to a very late tertiary period. From the bones of the Scelidotherium including even the knee-cap, being entombed in their proper relative positions, and from the osseous armour of the great armadillo-like animal being so well preserved, together with the bones of one of its legs, we may feel assured that these remains were fresh and united by their ligaments, when deposited in the gravel together with the shells. Hence we have good evidence that the above enumerated gigantic quadrupeds, more different from those of the present day than the oldest of the tertiary quadrupeds of Europe, lived whilst the sea was peopled with most of its present inhabitants; and we have confirmed that remarkable law so often insisted on by Mr Lyell [see p. 166], namely, that the 'longevity of the species in the mammalia is upon the whole inferior to that of the testacea'.

The great size of the bones of the megatheroid animals, including the Megatherium, Megalonyx, Scelidotherium, and Mylodon, is truly wonderful. The habits of life of these animals were a complete puzzle to naturalists, until Professor Owen lately solved the problem with remarkable ingenuity. The teeth indicate, by their simple structure, that these megatheroid animals lived on vegetable food, and probably on the leaves and small twigs of trees; their ponderous forms and great strong curved claws seem so little adapted for locomotion, that some eminent naturalists have actually believed, that, like the sloths, to which they are intimately related, they subsisted by climbing back-downwards on trees, and feeding on the leaves. It was a bold, not to say preposterous idea to conceive even an antediluvian tree, with branches strong enough to bear animals as large as elephants. Professor Owen, with far more probability, believes that, instead of climbing on the trees, they pulled the branches down to them, and tore up the smaller ones by the roots, and so fed on the leaves. The colossal breadth and weight of their hinder quarters, which can hardly be imagined without having been seen, become, on this view, of obvious service, instead of being an incumbrance: their apparent clumsiness disappears. With their great tails and their huge heels firmly fixed like a tripod on the ground, they could freely exert the full force of their most powerful arms and great claws. Strongly rooted, indeed, must that tree have been, which could have resisted such force! The Mylodon, moreover, was furnished with a long extensile tongue like that of the giraffe, which, by one of those beautiful provisions of nature, thus reaches with the aid of its long neck its leafy food. . . .

That large animals require a luxuriant vegetation has been a general assumption which has passed from one work to another; but I do not hesitate to say that it is completely false, and that it has vitiated the reasoning of geologists on some points of great interest in the ancient history of the world. The prejudice has probably been derived from India, and the Indian islands, where troops of elephants, noble forests, and impenetrable jungles, are associated together in every one's mind. If, however, we refer to any work of travels through the southern parts of Africa, we shall find allusions in almost every page either to the desert character of the country, or to the numbers of large animals inhabiting it. The same thing is rendered evident by the many engravings which have been published of various parts of the interior. When the *Beagle* was at Cape Town [May–June 1836], I made an excursion of some days' length into the country, which at least was sufficient to render that which I had read more fully intelligible....

If we look to the animals inhabiting these wide plains, we shall find their numbers extraordinarily great, and their bulk immense. We must enumerate the elephant, three species of rhinoceros, and probably, according to Dr Andrew Smith [African explorer], two others, the hippopotamus, the giraffe, the bos caffer (as large as a full-grown bull), and the elan (but little less), two zebras, and the quaccha [quagga], two gnus, and several antelopes even larger than these latter animals. It may be supposed that although the species are numerous, the individuals of each kind are few. By the kindness of Dr Smith, I am enabled to show that the case is very different. He informs me, that in lat. 24°, in one day's march with the bullock-wagons, he saw, without wandering to any great distance on either side, between 100 and 150 rhinoceroses, which belonged to three species. The same day he saw several herds of giraffes, amounting together to nearly a hundred; and that, although no elephant was observed, yet they are found in this district....

A very singular little bird, Tinochorus rumicivorus, is here common: in its habits and general appearance, it nearly equally partakes of the characters, different as they are, of the quail and snipe. The tinochorus is found in the whole of southern South America, wherever there are sterile plains, or open, dry pasture land. It frequents in pairs or small flocks the most desolate places, where scarcely another living creature can exist. Upon being approached they squat close, and then are very difficult to be distinguished from the ground. When feeding they walk rather slowly, with their legs wide apart. They dust themselves in roads and sandy places, and frequent particular spots, where they may be found day after day: like partridges, they take wing in a flock. In all these respects, in the muscular gizzard adapted for vegetable food, in the arched beak and fleshy nostrils, short legs and form of foot, the tinochorus has a close affinity with

The vegetation is scanty; and although there are bushes of many kinds, all are armed with formidable thorns, which seem to warn the stranger not to enter these inhospitable regions. (p. 63)

Flamingoes in considerable numbers inhabit this lake, and breed here . . . I saw them wading about in search of food. (p. 64)

A very singular little bird, Tinochorus rumicivorus, is here common. (p. 72)

. . . The little owl of the Pampas . . . which has so often been described as standing like a sentinel at the mouth of the burrows . . .(p. 65)

MELANOPHRYNISCUS SELZNERI

... I found only one little toad (Phryniscus nigricans), which was most singular from its colour. If we imagine, first, that it had been steeped in the blackest ink, and then, when dry, allowed to crawl over a board, freshly painted with the brightest vermilion, so as to colour the soles of its feet and parts of its stomach, a good idea of its appearance will be gained. (p. 77)

The Agouti [Mara] is a true friend of the desert; it is a common feature in the landscape to see two or three hopping quickly in a straight line. (p. 65)

MARA DOLICHOTIS AUSTRALIS

VULTUR GRYPHUS

The condors may oftentimes be seen at a great height, soaring over a certain spot in the most graceful circles . . . it is truly wonderful and beautiful to see so great a bird, hour after hour, without any apparent exertion, wheeling and gliding over mountain and river. (p. 88)

MICROCAVIA AUSTRALIS

Patagonia . . . can boast of a greater stock of small rodents (left) *than perhaps any other country in the world.* (p. 85)

The guanaco (below) *is also in his proper district: herds of fifty or a hundred were common.* (p. 85)

LAMA HUANACOS

quails. But as soon as the bird is seen flying, its whole appearance changes; the long pointed wings, so different from those in the gallinaceous order, the irregular manner of flight, and plaintive cry uttered at the moment of rising, recall the idea of a snipe. The sportsmen of the *Beagle* unanimously called it the short-billed snipe. To this genus, or rather to the family of the waders, its skeleton shows that it is really related. . . .

Of reptiles there are many kinds: one snake (a Trigonocephalus, or Cophias), from the size of the poison channel in its fangs, must be very deadly. Cuvier, in opposition to some other naturalists, makes this a sub-genus of the rattle-snake, and intermediate between it and the viper. In confirmation of this opinion, I observed a fact, which appears to me very curious and instructive, as showing how every character, even though it may be in some degree independent of structure, has a tendency to vary by slow degrees. The extremity of the tail of this snake is terminated by a point, which is very slightly enlarged; and as the animal glides along, it constantly vibrates the last inch; and this part striking against the dry grass and brushwood, produces a rattling noise, which can be distinctly heard at the distance of six feet. As often as the animal was irritated or surprised, its tail was shaken; and the vibrations were extremely rapid. Even as long as the body retained its irritability, a tendency to this habitual movement was evident. This trigonocephalus has, therefore, in some respects the structure of a viper, with the habits of a rattlesnake, the noise, however, being produced by a simpler device. The expression of this snake's face was hideous and fierce; the pupil consisted of a vertical slit in a mottled and coppery iris; the jaws were broad at the base, and the nose terminated in a triangular projection. I do not think I ever saw any thing more ugly, excepting, perhaps, some of the vampire bats. I imagine this repulsive aspect originates from the features being placed in positions, with respect to each other, somewhat proportional to those of the human face, and thus we obtain a scale of hideousness.

Amongst the Batrachian reptiles, I found only one little toad (Phryniscus nigricans), which was most singular from its colour. If we imagine, first, that it had been steeped in the blackest ink, and then, when dry, allowed to crawl over a board, freshly painted with the brightest vermilion, so as to colour the soles of its feet and parts of its stomach, a good idea of its appearance will be gained. If it had been an unnamed species, surely it ought to have been called 'Diabolicus', for it is a fit toad to preach in the ear of Eve. . . .

During my stay at Bahía Blanca, while waiting for the *Beagle*, the place was in a constant state of excitement from rumours of wars and victories between the troops of Rosas and the wild Indians. One day an account came that a small party forming one of the postas on the line to Buenos Aires had been found all murdered. The next day 300 men arrived from the Colorado, under the command of Commandant Miranda. A large portion of these men were Indians ('mansos', or tame), belonging to the tribe of the Cacique Bernantio. They passed the night here; and it was impossible to conceive any thing more wild and savage than the scene of their bivouac. Some drank till they were intoxicated; others swallowed the steaming blood of the cattle slaughtered for their suppers, and then, being sick from drunkenness, they cast it up again, and were besmeared with filth and gore....

In the morning they started for the scene of the murder, with orders to follow the 'rastro', or track, even if it led them to Chile. We subsequently heard that the wild Indians had escaped into the great pampas, and from some cause the track had been missed. One glance at the rastro tells these people a whole history. Supposing they examine the track of a thousand horses, they will soon guess the number of mounted ones by seeing how many have cantered; by the depth of the other impressions, whether any horses were loaded with cargoes; by the irregularity of the footsteps, how far tired; by the manner in which the food has been cooked, whether the pursued travelled in haste; by the general appearance, how long it has been since they passed. They consider a rastro of ten days or a fortnight, quite recent enough to be hunted out....

A few days afterwards I saw another troop of these banditti-like soldiers start on an expedition against a tribe of Indians at the small Salinas, who had been betrayed by a prisoner cacique. The Spaniard who brought the orders for this expedition was a very intelligent man. He gave me an account of the last engagement at which he was present. Some Indians, who had been taken prisoners, gave information of a tribe living north of the Colorado. Two hundred soldiers were sent; and they first discovered the Indians by a cloud of dust from their horses' feet, as they chanced to be travelling. The country was mountainous and wild, and it must have been far in the interior, for the Cordillera were in sight. The Indians, men, women and children, were about 110 in number, and they were nearly all taken or killed, for the soldiers sabre every man.

The Indians are now so terrified that they offer no resistance in a body, but each flies, neglecting even his wife and children; but when overtaken, like wild animals, they fight against any number to the last moment. One dying Indian seized with his teeth the thumb of his adversary, and allowed his own eye to be forced out sooner than relinquish his hold. Another, who was wounded, feigned death, keeping a knife ready to strike one more fatal blow. My informer said, when he was pursuing an Indian, the man cried out for mercy, at the same time that he was covertly loosing the bolas from his waist, meaning to whirl it round his head and so strike his pursuer. 'I however struck him with my sabre to the ground, and then got off my horse, and cut his throat with my knife.' This is a dark picture; but how much more shocking is the unquestionable fact, that all the women who appear above twenty years old are massacred in cold blood! When I exclaimed that this appeared rather inhuman, he answered, 'Why, what can be done? They breed so!'

Every one here is fully convinced that this is the most just war, because it is against barbarians. Who would believe in this age that such atrocities could be committed in a Christian civilised country? The children of the Indians are saved, to be sold or given away as servants, or rather slaves, for as long a time as the owners can make them believe themselves slaves; but I believe in their treatment there is little to complain of.

In the battle four men ran away together. They were pursued, one was killed, and the other three were taken alive. They turned out to be messengers or ambassadors from a large body of Indians, united in the common cause of defence near the Cordillera. The tribe to which they had been sent was on the point of holding a grand council. The feast of mare's flesh was ready, and the dance prepared; in the morning the ambassadors were to have returned to the Cordillera.

They were remarkably fine men, very fair, above six feet high, and all under thirty years of age. The three survivors, of course, possessed very valuable information, and to extort this they were placed in a line. The two first being questioned, answered, 'No sé' (I do not know), and were one after the other shot. The third also said 'No sé' adding, 'Fire, I am a man and can die!' Not one syllable would they breathe to injure the united cause of their country! The conduct of the above-mentioned cacique was very different. He saved his life by betraying the intended plan of warfare, and the point of union in the Andes. It was believed that there were already six or seven hundred Indians together, and that in summer their numbers would be doubled. Ambassadors were to have been sent to the Indians at the small salinas, near Bahia Blanca, whom I have mentioned that this same cacique had betrayed. The communication, therefore, between the Indians, extends from the Cordillera to the coast of the Atlantic.

General Rosas's plan is to kill all stragglers, and having driven the remainder to a common point, to attack them in a body, in the summer, with the assistance of the Chilenos. This operation is to be repeated for three successive years. I imagine the summer is chosen as the time for the main attack, because the plains are then without water, and the Indians can only travel in particular directions. The escape of the Indians to the south of the Rio Negro, where in such a vast unknown country they would be safe, is prevented by a treaty with the Tehuelches to this effect: that Rosas pays them so much to slaughter every Indian who passes to the south of the river, but if they fail in so doing, they themselves are to be exterminated. The war is waged chiefly against the Indians near the Cordillera; for many of the tribes on this eastern side are fighting with Rosas. The general, however, like Lord Chesterfield, thinking that his friends may in a future day become his enemies, always places them in the front ranks, so that their numbers may be thinned. Since leaving South America we have heard that this war of extermination completely failed.

Among the captive girls taken in the same engagement, there were two very pretty Spanish ones, who had been carried away by the Indians when young, and could now only speak the Indian tongue. From their account they must have come from Salta, a distance in a straight line of nearly one thousand miles. This gives one a grand idea of the immense territory over which the Indians roam: yet, great as it is, I think there will not, in another half century, be a wild Indian northward of the Rio Negro. The warfare is too bloody to last; the Christians killing every Indian, and the Indians doing the same by the Christians. . . .

It is impossible to reflect on the changed state of the American continent without the deepest astonishment. Formerly it must have swarmed with great monsters: now we find mere pygmies, compared with the antecedent, allied races. If Buffon had known of the gigantic sloth and armadillo-like animals, and of the lost pachydermata, he might have said with a greater semblance of truth that the creative force in America had lost its power, rather than that it had never possessed great vigour. The greater number, if not all, of these extinct quadrupeds lived at a late period, and were the contemporaries of most of the existing sea-shells. Since they lived, no very great change in the form of the land can have taken place. What, then, has exterminated so many species and whole genera? The mind at first is irresistibly hurried into the belief of some great catastrophe; but thus to destroy animals, both large and small, in Southern Patagonia, in Brazil, on the Cordillera of Peru, in North America up to Behring's Straits, we must shake the entire framework of the globe. An examination, moreover, of the geology of La Plata and Patagonia, leads to the belief that all the features of the land result from slow and gradual changes. It appears from the character of the fossils in Europe, Asia, Australia, and in North and South America, that those conditions which favour the life of the *larger* quadrupeds were lately co-extensive with the world: what those conditions were, no one has yet even conjectured. It could hardly have been a change of temperature, which at about the same time destroyed the inhabitants of tropical, temperate, and arctic latitudes on both sides of the globe. In North America we positively know from Mr Lyell, that the large quadrupeds lived subsequently to that period, when boulders were brought into latitudes at which icebergs now never arrive: from conclusive but indirect reasons we may feel sure, that in the southern hemisphere the Macrauchenia, also, lived long subsequently to the ice-transporting boulder-period.

Did man, after his first inroad into South America, destroy, as has been suggested, the unwieldy megatherium and the other edentata? We must at least look to some other cause for the destruction of the little tucutuco at Bahía Blanca, and of the many fossil mice and other small quadrupeds in Brazil. No one will imagine that a drought, even far severer than those which cause such losses in the provinces of La Plata, could destroy every individual of every species from Southern Patagonia to Behring's Straits. What shall we say of the extinction of the horse? Did those plains fail of pasture, which have since been overrun by thousands and hundreds of thousands of the descendants of the stock introduced by the Spaniards? Have the subsequently introduced species consumed the food of the great antecedent races? Can we believe that the capybara has taken the food of the toxodon, the guanaco of the macrauchenia, the existing small edentata of their numerous gigantic prototypes? Certainly, no fact in the long history of the world is so startling as the wide and repeated exterminations of its inhabitants.

Nevertheless, if we consider the subject under another point of view, it will appear less perplexing. We do not steadily bear in mind how profoundly ignorant we are of the conditions of existence of every animal; nor do we always remember, that some check is constantly preventing the too-rapid increase of every organised being left in a state of nature. The supply of food, on an average, remains constant; yet the tendency in every animal to increase by propagation is geometrical; and its surprising effects have nowhere been more astonishingly shown, than in the case of the European animals run wild during the last few centuries in America. Every animal in a state of nature regularly breeds; yet in a species long established, any *great* increase in numbers is obviously impossible, and must be checked by some means. We are, nevertheless, seldom able with certainty to tell in any given species, at what period of life, or at what period of the year, or whether only at long intervals, the check falls; or, again, what is the precise nature of the check. Hence probably it is that we feel so little surprise at one, of two species closely allied in habits, being rare and the other abundant in the same district; or, again, that one should be abundant in one district, and another, filling the same place in the economy of nature, should be abundant in a neighbouring district, differing very little in its conditions. If asked how this is, one immediately replies that it is determined by some slight difference in climate, food, or the number of enemies: yet how rarely, if ever, we can point out the precise cause and manner of action of the check! We are, therefore, driven to the conclusion, that causes generally quite inappreciable by us, determine whether a given species shall be abundant or scanty in numbers.

In the cases where we can trace the extinction of a species through man, either wholly or in one limited district, we know that it becomes rarer and rarer, and is then lost: it would be difficult to point out any just distinction between a species destroyed by man or by the increase of its natural enemies. The evidence of rarity preceding extinction, is more striking in the successive tertiary strata, as remarked by several able observers; it has often been found that a shell very common in a tertiary stratum is now most rare, and has even long been thought to be extinct. If then, as appears probable, species first become rare and then extinct – if the too rapid increase of every species, even the most favoured, is steadily checked, as we must admit, though how and when it is hard to say – and if we see, without the smallest surprise, though unable to assign the precise reason, one species abundant and another closely-allied species rare in the same district – why should we feel such great astonishment at the rarity being carried a step further to extinction? An action going on, on every side of us, and yet barely appreciable, might surely be carried a little further, without exciting our observation. Who would feel any great surprise at hearing that the megalonyx was formerly rare compared with the megatherium, or that one of the fossil monkeys was few in number compared with one of the now living monkeys? And yet in this comparative rarity we should have the plainest evidence of less favourable conditions for their existence. To admit that species generally become rare before they become extinct – to feel no surprise at the comparative rarity of one species with another, and yet to call in some extraordinary agent and to marvel greatly when a species ceases to exist, appears to me much the same as to admit that sickness in the individual is the prelude to death – to feel no surprise at sickness – but when the sick man dies, to wonder, and to believe that he died through violence.

[*The end of 1833 was spent based at Montevideo, and at the turn of the year the* Beagle *moved to Port Desire in Patagonia. By April 1834 she had visited the Falkland Islands and, for the second time, Tierra del Fuego. The visit to Port Desire cost them some damage to the* Beagle, *to repair which they called in at the mouth of the Santa Cruz river, and while the repairs went ahead the following expedition up-river was undertaken:*]

PATAGONIA: JOURNEY UP THE SANTA CRUZ RIVER, 13 APRIL TO 8 MAY 1834

JOURNAL 13 APRIL

The *Beagle* anchored within the mouth of the Santa Cruz. This river is situated about sixty miles south of Port St Julian. During the last voyage Captain Stokes proceeded thirty miles up it, but then from the want of provisions, was obliged to return. Excepting what was discovered at that time, scarcely anything was known about this large river. Captain FitzRoy now determined to follow its course as far as time would allow. On the 18th three whale-boats started, carrying three weeks' provisions; and the party consisted of twenty-five souls – a force which would have been sufficient to have defied a host of Indians. With a strong flood-tide and a fine day we made a good run, soon drank some of the fresh water, and were at night nearly above the tidal influence.

The river here assumed a size and appearance which, even at the highest point we ultimately reached, was scarcely diminished. It was generally from three to four hundred yards broad, and in the middle about seventeen feet deep. The rapidity of the current, which in its whole course runs at the rate of from four to six knots an hour, is perhaps its most remarkable feature. The water is of a fine blue colour, but with a slight milky tinge, and not so transparent as at first sight would have been expected. It flows over a bed of pebbles, like those which compose the beach and the surrounding plains. It runs in a winding course through a valley, which extends in a direct line westward. This valley varies from five to ten miles in breadth; it is bounded by step-formed terraces, which rise in most parts, one above the other, to the height of five hundred feet, and have on the opposite sides a remarkable correspondence.

19 APRIL

Against so strong a current it was, of course, quite impossible to row or sail: consequently the three boats were fastened together head and stern, two hands left in each, and the rest came on shore to track. . . . The party, including every one, was divided into two spells, each of which hauled at the tracking line alternately for an hour and a half. The officers of each boat lived with, ate the same food, and slept in the same tent with their crew, so that each boat was quite independent of the others. After sunset the first level spot where any bushes were growing was chosen for our night's lodging. Each of the crew took it in turns to be cook. Immediately the boat was hauled up, the cook made his fire; two others pitched the tent; the coxswain handed the things out of the boat; the rest carried them up to the tents and collected firewood. By this order, in half an hour everything was ready for the night. A watch of two men and an officer was always kept, whose duty it was to look after the boats, keep up the fire, and guard against Indians. Each in the party had his one hour every night.

During this day we tracked but a short distance, for there were many islets, covered by thorny bushes, and the channels between them were shallow.

20 APRIL

We passed the islands and set to work. Our regular day's march, although it was hard enough, carried us on an average only ten miles in a straight line, and perhaps fifteen or twenty altogether. Beyond the place where we slept last night, the country is completely *terra incognita*, for it was there that Captain Stokes turned back. We saw in the distance a great smoke, and found the skeleton of a horse, so we knew that Indians were in the neighbourhood. On the next morning (21st) tracks of a party of horse, and marks left by the trailing of the chuzos, or long spears, were observed on the ground. It was generally thought that the Indians had reconnoitred us during the night. Shortly afterwards we came to a spot where, from the fresh footsteps of men, children and horses it was evident that the party had crossed the river.

The country remained the same, and extremely uninteresting. The complete similarity of the productions throughout Patagonia is one of its most striking characters. The level plains of arid shingle support the same stunted and dwarf plants, and in the valleys the same thorn-bearing bushes grow. Everywhere we see the same birds and insects. Even the very banks of the river and of the clear stream-lets which entered it, were scarcely enlivened by a brighter tint of green. The curse of sterility is on the land, and the water flowing over a bed of pebbles partakes of the same curse. Hence the number of waterfowl is very scanty; for there is nothing to support life in the stream of this barren river.

Patagonia, poor as she is in some respects, can however, boast of a greater stock of small rodents than perhaps any other country in the world. Several species of mice are externally characterised by large thin ears and a very fine fur. These little animals swarm amongst the thickets in the valleys, where they cannot for months together taste a drop of water excepting the dew. They all seem to be cannibals, for no sooner was a mouse caught in one of my traps than it was devoured by others. A small and delicately-shaped fox, which is likewise very abundant, probably derives its entire support from these small animals. The guanaco is also in his proper district: herds of fifty or a hundred were common, and, as I have stated, we saw one which must have contained at least 500. The puma, with the condor and other carrion-hawks in its train, follows and preys upon these animals. The footsteps of the puma were to be seen almost everywhere on the banks of the river; and the remains of several guanacos, with their necks dislocated and bones broken, showed how they had met their death.

Like the navigators of old when approaching an unknown land, we examined and watched for the most trivial sign of a change. The drifted trunk of a tree, or a boulder or primitive rock, was hailed with joy, as if we had seen a forest growing on the flanks of the Cordillera. The top, however, of a heavy bank of clouds, which remained almost constantly in one position, was the most promising sign, and eventually turned out a true harbinger. At first the clouds were mistaken for the mountains themselves, instead of the masses of vapour condensed by their icy summits.

We this day met with a marked change in the geological structure of the plains. From the first starting I had carefully examined the gravel in the river, and for the two last days had noticed the presence of a few small pebbles of a very cellular basalt. These gradually increased in number and in size, but none were as large as a man's head. This morning, however, pebbles of the same rock, but more compact, suddenly became abundant, and in the course of half an hour we saw, at the distance of five or six miles, the angular edge of a great basaltic platform. When we arrived at its base we found the stream bubbling among the fallen blocks. For the next twenty-eight miles the river-course was encumbered with these basaltic masses. Above that limit immense fragments of primitive rocks, derived from the surrounding boulder-formation, were equally numerous. None of the fragments of any considerable size had been washed more than three or four miles down the river below their parent-source: considering the singular rapidity of the great body of water in the Santa Cruz, and that no still reaches occur in any part, this example is a most striking one of the inefficiency of rivers in transporting even moderately-sized fragments.

The basalt is only lava, which has flowed beneath the sea; but the eruptions must have been on the grandest scale. At the point where we first met this formation, it was 120 feet in thickness; following up the river-course, the surface imperceptibly rose and the mass became thicker, so that at forty miles above the first station it was 320 feet thick. What the thickness may be close to the Cordillera, I have no means of knowing, but the platform there attains a height of about 3000 feet above the level of the sea: we must therefore look to the mountains of that great chain for its source; and worthy of such a source are streams that have flowed over the gently-inclined bed of the sea to a distance of 100 miles. At the first glance of the basaltic cliffs on the opposite sides of the valley, it was evident that the strata once were united. What power, then, had removed along a whole line of country, a solid mass of very hard rock, which had an average thickness of nearly three hundred feet, and a breadth varying from rather less than two miles to four miles? The river, though it has so little power in transporting even inconsiderable fragments, yet in the lapse of ages might produce by its gradual erosion an effect of which it is difficult to judge the amount. But in this case, independently of the insignificance of such an agency, good reasons can be assigned for believing that this valley was formerly occupied by an arm of the sea. It is needless in this work to detail the arguments leading to this conclusion, derived from the form and the nature of the step-formed terraces on both sides of the valley, from the manner in which the bottom of the valley near the Andes expands into a great estuary-like plain with sand-hillocks on it, and from the occurrence of a few sea-shells lying in the bed of the river. If I had space I could prove that South America was formerly here cut off by a strait, joining the Atlantic and Pacific oceans, like that of Magellan.

But it may yet be asked, how has the solid basalt been removed? Geologists formerly would have brought into play, the violent action of some overwhelming débâcle. But in this case such a supposition would have been quite inadmissible, because, the same step-like plains with existing seashells lying on their surface, which front the long line of the Patagonian coast, sweep up on each side of the valley of Santa Cruz. No possible action of any flood could thus have modelled the land, either within the valley or along the open coast; and by the formation of such step-like plains or terraces the valley itself has been hollowed out. Although we know that there are tides which run within the narrows of the Strait of Magellan at the rate of eight knots an hour, yet we must confess that it makes the head almost giddy to reflect on the number of years, century after century, which the tides, unaided by a heavy surf, must have required to have corroded so vast an area and thickness of solid basaltic lava. Nevertheless, we must believe that the strata undermined by the waters of this ancient strait, were broken up into huge fragments, and these lying scattered in the beach, were reduced first to smaller blocks, then to pebbles, and lastly to the most impalpable mud, which the tides drifted far into the eastern or western ocean.

With the change in the geological structure of the plains the character of the landscape likewise altered. While rambling up some of the narrow and rocky defiles, I could almost have fancied myself transported back again to the barren valleys of the island of São Tiago [in the Cape Verde Islands]. Among the basaltic cliffs, I found some plants which I had seen nowhere else, but others I recognised as being wanderers from Tierra del Fuego. These porous rocks serve as a reservoir for the scanty rain-water, and consequently on the line where the igneous and sedimentary formations unite, some small springs (most rare occurrences in Patagonia) burst forth. They could be distinguished at a distance by the circumscribed patches of bright green herbage.

The bed of the river became rather narrower, and hence the stream more rapid. It here ran at the rate of six knots an hour. From this cause, and from the many great angular fragments, tracking the boats became both dangerous and laborious.

This day I shot a condor. It measured from tip to tip of the wings, eight and a half feet, and from beak to tail, four feet. This bird is known to have a wide geographical range, being found on the west coast of South America, from the Strait of Magellan along the Cordillera as far as eight degrees north of the equator.... A line of cliff near the mouth of the Santa Cruz is frequented by these birds, and about eighty miles up the river, where the sides of the valley are formed by steep basaltic precipices, the condor reappears. From these facts, it seems that the condors require perpendicular cliffs. In Chile they haunt, during the greater part of the year, the lower country near the shores of the Pacific, and at night several roost together in one tree; but in the early part of summer they return to the most inaccessible parts of the inner Cordillera, there to breed in peace....

The condors may oftentimes be seen at a great height, soaring over a certain spot in the most graceful circles. On some occasions I am sure that they do this only for pleasure, but on others, the Chileno countryman tells you that they are watching a dying animal, or the puma devouring its prey. If the condors glide down, and then suddenly all rise together, the Chileno knows that it is the puma which, watching the carcass, has sprung out to drive away the robbers. Besides feeding on carrion, the condors frequently attack young goats and lambs, and the shepherd dogs are trained, whenever they pass over, to run out, and looking upwards to bark violently. The Chilenos destroy and catch numbers....

When the condors are wheeling in a flock round and round any spot, their flight is beautiful. Except when rising from the ground, I do not recollect ever having seen one of these birds flap its wings. Near Lima, I watched several for nearly half an hour, without once taking off my eyes: they moved in large curves, sweeping in circles, descending and ascending without giving a single flap. As they glided close over my head, I intently watched from an oblique position, the outlines of the separate and great terminal feathers of each wing; and these separate feathers, if there had been the least vibratory movement, would have appeared as if blended together; but they were seen distinct against the blue sky. The head and neck were moved frequently, and apparently with force; and the extended wings seemed to form the fulcrum on which the movements of the neck, body, and tail acted. If the bird wished to descend, the wings were for a moment collapsed; and when again expanded with an altered inclination, the momentum gained by the rapid descent seemed to urge the bird upwards with the even and steady movement of a paper kite. In the case of any bird *soaring*, its motion must be sufficiently rapid, so that the action of the inclined surface of its body on the atmosphere may counter balance its gravity. The force to keep up the momentum of a body moving in a horizontal plane in the air (in which there is no little friction) cannot be great, and this force is all that is wanted. The movement of the neck and body of the condor, we must suppose, is sufficient for this. However this may be, it is truly wonderful and beautiful to see so great a bird, hour after hour, without any apparent exertion, wheeling and gliding over mountain and river.

29 APRIL

From some high land we hailed with joy the white summits of the Cordillera, as they were seen occasionally peeping through their dusky envelope of clouds. During the few succeeding days we continued to get on slowly, for we found the river-course very tortuous, and strewed with immense fragments of various ancient slaty rocks, and of granite. The plain bordering the valley had here attained an elevation of about 1100 feet above the river, and its character was much altered. The well-rounded pebbles of porphyry were mingled with many immense angular fragments of basalt and of primary rocks. The first of these erratic boulders which I noticed, was sixty-seven miles distant from the nearest mountain; another which I measured was five yards square, and projected five feet above the gravel. Its edges were so angular, and its size so great, that I at first mistook it for a rock *in situ*, and took out my compass to observe the direction of its cleavage. The plain here was not quite so level as that nearer the coast, but yet it betrayed no signs of any great violence. Under these circumstances it is, I believe, quite impossible to explain the transportal of these gigantic masses of rock so many miles from their parent-source, on any theory except by that of floating icebergs. . . .

4 MAY

Captain FitzRoy determined to take the boats no higher. The river had a winding course, and was very rapid, and the appearance of the country offered no temptation to proceed any further. Everywhere we met with the same productions, and the same dreary landscape. We were now 140 miles distant from the Atlantic, and about sixty from the nearest arm of the Pacific. The valley in this upper part expanded into a wide basin, bounded on the north and south by the basaltic platforms, and fronted by the long range of the snow-clad Cordillera. But we viewed these grand mountains with regret, for we were obliged to imagine their nature and productions, instead of standing, as we had hoped, on their summits. Besides the useless loss of time which an attempt to ascend the river any higher would have cost us, we had already been for some days on half-allowance of bread. This, although really enough for reasonable men, was, after a hard day's march, rather scanty food: a light stomach and an easy digestion are good things to talk about, but very unpleasant in practice.

5 MAY

Before sunrise we commenced our descent. We shot down the stream with great rapidity, generally at the rate of ten knots an hour. In this one day we effected what had cost us five and a half hard days' labour in ascending. On the 8th, we reached the *Beagle* after our twenty-one days' expedition. Every one, excepting myself, had cause to be dissatisfied; but to me the ascent afforded a most interesting section of the great tertiary formation of Patagonia.

[*As has been explained, the Tierra del Fuego episodes which follow were placed together by Darwin in the Journal, so that the reader could follow the experience in one section. The Diary, of course, remains chronological, and consequently somewhat disjointed; so, with the exception of the rounding of Cape Horn, which is more graphic in the Diary, we have followed the same narrative layout as Darwin chose for the Journal. The reader should bear in mind that there was a lapse of a full year between the first visit to Woollya Cove and the second, during which the* Beagle *returned to the Atlantic.*]

Tierra del Fuego

Having now finished with Patagonia, I will describe our first arrival in Tierra del Fuego. A little after noon we doubled Cape St Diego, and entered the famous Strait of Le Maire. We kept close to the Fuegian shore, but the outline of the rugged, inhospitable Staten-land was visible amidst the clouds. In the afternoon we anchored in the Bay of Good Success. While entering we were saluted in a manner becoming the inhabitants of this savage land. A group of Fuegians partly concealed by the entangled forest, were perched on a wild point overhanging the sea; and as we passed by, they sprang up and, waving their tattered cloaks, sent forth a loud and sonorous shout. The savages followed the ship, and just before dark we saw their fire, and again heard their wild cry. The harbour consists of a fine piece of water half-surrounded by low, rounded mountains of clay-slate, which are covered to the water's edge by one dense gloomy forest. A single glance at the landscape was sufficient to show me how widely different it was from any thing I had ever beheld. At night it blew a gale of wind, and heavy squalls from the mountains swept past us. It would have been a bad time out at sea, and we, as well as others, may call this Good Success Bay.

In the morning the Captain sent a party to communicate with the Fuegians. When we came within hail, one of the four natives who were present advanced to receive us, and began to shout most vehemently, wishing to direct us where to land. When we were on shore the party looked rather alarmed, but continued talking and making gestures with great rapidity. It was without exception the most curious and interesting spectacle I ever beheld: I could not have believed how wide was the difference between savage and civilised man: it is greater than between a wild and domesticated animal, inasmuch as in man there is a greater power of improvement.

The chief spokesman was old, and appeared to be the head of the family; the three others were powerful young men, about six feet high. The women and children had been sent away. These Fuegians are a very different race from the stunted, miserable wretches farther westward; and they seem closely allied to the famous Patagonians of the Strait of Magellan. Their only garment consists of a mantle made of guanaco skin, with the wool outside; this they wear just thrown over their shoulders, leaving their persons as often exposed as covered. Their skin is of a dirty coppery-red colour.

The old man had a fillet of white feathers tied round his head, which partly confined his black, coarse, and entangled hair. His face was crossed by two broad transverse bars; one, painted bright red, reached from ear to ear and included the upper lip; the other, white like chalk, extended above and parallel to the first, so that even his eyelids were thus coloured. The other two men were ornamented by streaks of black powder, made of charcoal. The party altogether closely resembled the devils which come on the stage in plays like *Der Freischütz*.

Their very attitudes were abject, and the expression of their countenances distrustful, surprised, and startled. After we had presented them with some scarlet cloth, which they immediately tied round their necks, they became good friends. This was shown by the old man patting our breasts, and making a chuckling kind of noise, as people do when feeding chickens. I walked with the old man, and this demonstration of friendship was repeated several times. It was concluded by three hard slaps, which were given me on the breast and back at the same time. He then bared his bosom for me to return the compliment, which being done, he seemed highly pleased. The language of these people, according to our notions, scarcely deserves to be called articulate. Captain Cook had compared it to a man clearing his throat, but certainly no European ever cleared his throat with so many hoarse, guttural, and clicking sounds.

They are excellent mimics: as often as we coughed or yawned, or made any odd motion, they immediately imitated us. Some of our party began to squint and look awry; but one of the young Fuegians (whose whole face was painted black, excepting a white band across his eyes) succeeded in making far more hideous grimaces. They could repeat with perfect correctness each word in any sentence we addressed them, and they remembered such words for some time. Yet we Europeans all know how difficult it is to distinguish apart the sounds in a foreign language. Which of us, for instance, could follow an American Indian through a sentence of more than three words? All savages appear to possess, to an uncommon degree, this power of mimicry. I was told, almost in the same words, of the same ludicrous habit among the Caffres [Kaffirs]: the Australians, likewise, have long been notorious for being able to imitate and describe the gait of any man, so that he may be recognised. How can this faculty be explained? Is it a consequence of the more practised habits of perception and keener senses, common to all men in a savage state, as compared with those long civilised?

When a song was struck up by our party, I thought the Fuegians would have fallen down with astonishment. With equal surprise they viewed our dancing; but one of the young men, when asked, had no objection to a little waltzing. Little accustomed to Europeans as they appeared to be, yet they knew and dreaded our fire-arms; nothing would tempt them to take a gun in their hands. They begged for knives, calling them by the Spanish word 'cuchilla'. They explained also what they wanted, by acting as if they had a piece of blubber in their mouth, and then pretending to cut instead of tear it.

I have not as yet noticed [mentioned] the Fuegians whom we had on board. During the former voyage of the *Adventure* and *Beagle* in 1826 to 1830, Captain FitzRoy seized on a party of natives, as hostages for the loss of a boat, which had been stolen, to the great jeopardy of a party employed on the survey; and some of these natives, as well as a child whom he bought for a pearl button, he took with him to England, determining to educate them and instruct them in religion at his own expense. To settle these natives in their own country, was one chief inducement to Captain FitzRoy to undertake our present voyage: and before the Admiralty had resolved to send out this expedition, Captain FitzRoy had generously chartered a vessel, and would himself have taken them back. The natives were accompanied by a missionary, R. Matthews, of whom and of the natives, Captain FitzRoy had published a full and excellent account.

Two men, one of whom died in England of the smallpox, a boy and a little girl, were originally taken; and we had now on board York Minster, Jemmy Button (whose name expresses his purchase-money), and Fuegia Basket. York Minster was a full-grown, short, thick, powerful man: his disposition was reserved, taciturn, morose, and when excited violently passionate. His affections were very strong towards a few friends on board, his intellect good. Jemmy Button was a universal favourite, but likewise passionate: the expression of his face at once showed his nice disposition. He was merry and often laughed, and was remarkably sympathetic with any one in pain. When the water was rough I was often a little sea-sick, and he used to come to me and say in a plaintive voice, 'Poor, poor fellow!' But the notion, after his aquatic life, of a man being sea-sick, was too ludicrous, and he was generally obliged to turn on one side to hide a smile or laugh, and then he would repeat his 'poor, poor fellow!' He was of a patriotic disposition; and he liked to praise his own tribe and country, in which he truly said were 'plenty of trees', and he abused all the other tribes: he stoutly declared that there was no Devil in his land.

Jemmy was short, thick, and fat, but vain of his personal appearance; he used to wear gloves, his hair was neatly cut, and he was distressed if his well-polished shoes were dirtied. He was fond of admiring himself in a looking-glass, and a merry-faced little Indian boy from the Rio Negro, whom we had for some months on board, soon perceived this, and used to mock him. Jemmy, who was always rather jealous of the attention paid to this little boy, did not at all like this, and used to say, with rather a contemptuous twist of his head, 'Too much skylark'. It seems yet wonderful to me, when I think over all his many good qualities, that he should have been of the same race, and doubtless partaken of the same character, with the miserable, degraded savages whom we first met here.

Lastly, Fuegia Basket was a nice, modest, reserved young girl, with a rather pleasing but sometimes sullen expression, and very quick in learning anything, especially languages. This she showed in picking up some Portuguese and Spanish, when left on shore for only a short time at Rio de Janeiro and Montevideo, and in her knowledge of English. York Minster was very jealous of any attention paid to her; for it was clear he determined to marry her as soon as they were settled on shore.

Although all three could both speak and understand a good deal of English, it was singularly difficult to obtain much information from them concerning the habits of their countrymen: this was partly owing to their apparent difficulty in understanding the simplest alternative. Every one accustomed to very young children, knows how seldom one can get an answer even to so simple a question as whether a thing is black *or* white. The idea of black or white seems alternately to fill their minds. So it was with these Fuegians, and hence it was generally impossible to find out, by cross-questioning, whether one had rightly understood anything which they had asserted. Their sight was remarkably acute. It is well known that sailors, from long practice, can make out a distant object much better than a landsman, but both York and Jemmy were much superior to any sailor on board: several times they have declared what some distant object has been, and though doubted by every one, they have proved right when it has been examined through a telescope. They were quite conscious of this power, and Jemmy, when he had any little quarrel with the officer on watch, would say, 'Me see ship, me no tell'.

It was interesting to watch the conduct of the savages, when we landed, towards Jemmy Button. They immediately perceived the difference between him and ourselves, and held much conversation one with another on the subject. The old man addressed a long harangue to Jemmy, which it seems was to invite him to stay with them. But Jemmy understood very little of their language, and was, moreover, thoroughly ashamed of his countrymen. When York Minster afterwards came on shore, they noticed him in the same way, and told him he ought to shave; yet he had not twenty dwarf hairs on his face, whilst we all wore our untrimmed beards. They examined the colour of his skin, and compared it with ours. One of our arms being bared, they expressed the liveliest surprise and admiration at its whiteness, just in the same way in which I have seen the orang-utang do at the Zoological Gardens. We thought that they mistook two or three of the officers, who were rather shorter and fairer, though adorned with large beards, for the ladies of our party. The tallest among the Fuegians was evidently much pleased at his height being noticed. When placed back to back with the tallest of the boat's crew, he tried his best to edge on higher ground, and to stand on tiptoe. He opened his mouth to show his teeth, and turned his face for a side view; and all this was done with such alacrity, that I dare say he thought himself the handsomest man in Tierra del Fuego. After our first feeling of grave astonishment was over, nothing could be more ludicrous than the odd mixture of surprise and imitation which these savages every moment exhibited.

The next day I attempted to penetrate some way into the country. Tierra del Fuego may be described as a mountainous land, partly submerged in the sea, so that deep inlets and bays occupy the place where valleys should exist. The mountain sides, except on the exposed western coast, are covered from the water's edge upwards by one great forest. The trees reach to an elevation of between 1000 and 1500 feet, and are succeeded by a band of peat, with minute alpine plants; and this again is succeeded by the line of perpetual snow, which, according to Captain King, in the Strait of Magellan descends to between 3000 and 4000 feet. To find an acre of level land in any part of the country is most rare. I recollect only one little flat piece near Port Famine, and another of rather larger extent near Goeree Road. In both places, and everywhere else, the surface is covered by a thick bed of swampy peat. Even within the forest, the ground is concealed by a mass of slowly putrefying vegetable matter, which, from being soaked with water, yields to the foot.

Finding it nearly hopeless to push my way through the wood, I followed the course of a mountain torrent. At first, from the waterfalls and number of dead trees, I could hardly crawl along; but the bed of the stream soon became a little more open, from the floods having swept the sides. I continued slowly to advance for an hour along the broken and rocky banks, and was amply repaid by the grandeur of the scene. The gloomy depth of the ravine well accorded with the universal signs of violence. On every side were lying irregular masses of rock and torn-up trees: other trees, though still erect, were decayed to the heart and ready to fall. The entangled mass of the thriving and the fallen reminded me of the forests within the tropics – yet there was a difference, for in these still solitudes, death, instead of life, seemed the predominant spirit. . . .

There was a degree of mysterious grandeur in mountain behind mountain, with the deep intervening valleys, all covered by one thick, dusky mass of forest. The atmosphere, likewise, in this climate, where gale succeeds gale, with rain, hail, and sleet, seems blacker than anywhere else. In the Strait of Magellan, looking due southward from Port Famine, the distant channels between the mountains appeared from their gloominess to lead beyond the confines of this world.

21 DECEMBER

The *Beagle* got under weigh, and on the succeeding day, favoured to an uncommon degree by a fine easterly breeze, we closed in with the Barnevelts, and running past Cape Deceit with its stony peaks, about three o'clock doubled the weather-beaten Cape Horn. The evening was calm and bright, and we enjoyed a fine view of the surrounding isles. Cape Horn, however, demanded his tribute, and before night sent us a gale of wind directly in our teeth. We stood out to sea, and on the second day again made the land, when we saw on our weather-bow this notorious promontory in its proper form – veiled in a mist, and its dim outline surrounded by a storm of wind and water. Great black clouds were rolling across the heavens, and squalls of rain, with hail, swept by us with such extreme violence that the Captain determined to run into Wigwam Cove. This is a snug little harbour, not far from Cape Horn: and here, at Christmas Eve, we anchored in smooth water. The only thing which reminded us of the gale outside, was every now and then a puff from the mountains, which made the ship surge at her anchors. . . .

While going one day on shore near Wollaston Island, we pulled alongside a canoe with six Fuegians. These were the most abject and miserable creatures I anywhere beheld. On the east coast the natives, as we have seen, have guanaco cloaks, and on the west, they possess seal-skins. Amongst these central tribes the men generally have an otter-skin, or some small scrap about as large as a pocket-handker-chief, which is barely sufficient to cover their backs as low down as their loins. It is laced across the breast by strings, and according as the wind blows, it is shifted from side to side. But these Fuegians in the canoe were quite naked, and even one full-grown woman was absolutely so. It was raining heavily, and the fresh water, together with the spray, trickled down her body.

In another harbour not far distant, a woman who was suckling a recently-born child came one day alongside the vessel, and remained there out of mere curiosity, whilst the sleet fell and thawed on her naked bosom, and on the skin of her naked baby! These poor wretches were stunted in their growth, their hideous faces bedaubed with white paint, their skins filthy and greasy, their hair entangled, their voices discordant, and their gestures violent. Viewing such men, one can hardly make oneself believe that they are fellow-creatures, and inhabitants of the same world. It is a common subject of conjecture what pleasure in life some of the lower animals can enjoy: how much more reasonably the same question may be asked with respect to these barbarians! At night, five or six human beings, naked and scarcely protected from the wind and rain of this tempes-tuous climate, sleep on the wet ground coiled up like animals. . . .

Mr Low [a sealing-master familiar with the country] believes that whenever a whale is cast on shore, the natives bury large pieces of it in the sand, as a resource in time of famine; and a native boy whom he had on board once found a stock thus buried. The different tribes when at war are cannibals. From the concurrent, but quite indepen-dent evidence of the boy taken by Mr Low, and of Jemmy Button, it is certainly true that, when pressed in winter by hunger, they kill and devour their old women before they kill their dogs: the boy, being asked by Mr Low why they did this, answered, 'Doggies catch otters, old women no'. This boy described the manner in which they are killed by being held over smoke and thus choked. He imitated their screams as a joke, and described the parts of their bodies which are considered best to eat. Horrid as such a death by the hands of their friends and relatives must be, the fears of the old women, when hunger begins to press, are more painful to think of. We were told that they then often run away into the mountains, but that they are pursued by the men and brought back to the slaughter-house at their own firesides!

Captain FitzRoy could never ascertain that the Fuegians have any distinct belief in a future life. They sometimes bury their dead in caves, and sometimes in the mountain forests. We do not know what ceremonies they perform. Jemmy Button would not eat land-birds, because 'eat dead men'. They are unwilling even to mention their dead friends. I do not think that our Fuegians were much more superstitious than some of the sailors, for an old quarter-master firmly believed that the successive heavy gales which we encountered off Cape Horn were caused by our having the Fuegians on board.

The different tribes have no government or chief, yet each is surrounded by other hostile tribes, speaking different dialects and separated from each other only by a deserted border or neutral territory. The cause of their warfare appears to be the means of subsistence. Their country is a broken mass of wild rocks, lofty hills and useless forests, and these are viewed through mists and endless storms. The habitable land is reduced to the stones on the beach. In search of food they are compelled unceasingly to wander from spot to spot, and so steep is the coast that they can only move about in their wretched canoes. They cannot know the feeling of having a home, and still less that of domestic affection, for the husband is to the wife a brutal master to a laborious slave. Was a more horrid deed ever perpetrated, than that witnessed on the west coast by Byron, who saw a wretched mother pick up her bleeding, dying infant-boy, whom her husband had mercilessly dashed on the stones for dropping a basket of sea-eggs! How little can the higher powers of the mind be brought into play. What is there for imagination to picture, for reason to compare, for judgment to decide upon? To knock a limpet from the rock does not require even cunning, that lowest power of the mind. Their skill in some respects may be compared to the instinct of animals, for it is not improved by experience: the canoe, their most ingenious work, poor as it is, has remained the same, as we know from Drake, for the last two hundred and fifty years.

Whilst beholding these savages one asks, whence have they come? What could have tempted, or what change compelled a tribe of men, to leave the fine regions of the north, to travel down the Cordillera or backbone of America, to invent and build canoes, which are not used by the tribes of Chile, Peru, and Brazil, and then to enter on one of the most inhospitable countries within the limits of the globe? Although such reflections must at first seize on the mind, yet we may feel sure that they are partly erroneous. There is no reason to believe that the Fuegians decrease in number: therefore we must suppose that they enjoy a sufficient share of happiness, of whatever kind it may be, to render life worth having. Nature, by making habit omnipotent and its effects hereditary, has fitted the Fuegian to the climate and the productions of his miserable country.

DIARY 9 JANUARY 1833

We doubled Cape Horn on the 21st, since which we have either been waiting for good, or beating against bad weather, and now we actually are about the same distance, viz. a hundred miles, from our destination. There is however the essential difference of being to the south instead of the east. Besides the serious and utter loss of time, and the necessary discomforts of the ship heavily pitching, and the miseries of constant wet and cold, I have scarcely for an hour been quite free from seasickness. How long the bad weather may last, I know not; but my spirits, temper and stomach, I am well assured, will not hold out much longer.

12 JANUARY

A gale with much rain: at night it freshened into a regular storm. The Captain was afraid it would have carried away the close-reefed main topsail. We then continued with merely the try-sails and storm staysail.

13 JANUARY

The gale does not abate: if the *Beagle* was not an excellent sea-boat, and our tackle in good condition, we should be in distress. A less gale has dismasted and foundered many a good ship. The worst part of the business is our not exactly knowing our position: it has an awkward sound to hear the officers repeatedly telling the lookout man to look well to leeward. Our horizon was limited to a small compass by the spray carried by the wind. The sea looked ominous: there was so much foam, that it resembled a dreary plain covered by patches of drifted snow. Whilst we were heavily labouring, it was curious to see how the albatross with its widely expanded wings, glided right up the wind.

At noon the storm was at its height, and we began to suffer. A great sea struck us and came on board; the after tackle of the quarter boat gave way and, an axe being obtained, they were instantly obliged to cut away one of the beautiful whaleboats. The same sea filled our decks so deep that if another had followed it is not difficult to guess the result. It is not easy to imagine what a state of confusion the decks were in from the great body of water. At last the ports were knocked open and she again rose buoyant to the sea.... Captain FitzRoy considers it the worst gale he was ever in.

15 JANUARY

The *Beagle* anchored in Goeree Roads. Captain FitzRoy having resolved to settle the Fuegians, according to their wishes, in Ponsonby Sound, four boats were equipped to carry them there through the Beagle Channel. This channel, which was discovered by Captain FitzRoy during the last voyage, is a most remarkable feature in the geography of this, or indeed of any other country: it may be compared to the valley of Loch Ness in Scotland, with its chain of lakes and friths. It is about 120 miles long, with an average breadth, not subject to any very great variation, of about two miles, and is throughout the greater part so perfectly straight that the view, bounded on each side by a line of mountains, gradually becomes indistinct in the long distance. It crosses the southern part of Tierra del Fuego in an east and west line, and in the middle is joined at right angles on the south side by an irregular channel, which has been called Ponsonby Sound. This is the residence of Jemmy Button's tribe and family.

19 JANUARY

Three whale-boats and the yawl, with a party of twenty-eight, started under the command of Captain FitzRoy....

20 JANUARY

The next day we ... came to a more inhabited district. Few if any of these natives could ever have seen a white man: certainly nothing could exceed their astonishment at the apparition of the four boats. Fires were lighted on every point (hence the name of Tierra del Fuego, or the land of fire), both to attract our attention and to spread far and wide the news. Some of the men ran for miles along the shore. I shall never forget how wild and savage one group appeared. Suddenly four or five men came to the edge of an overhanging cliff: they were absolutely naked, and their long hair streamed about their faces; they held rugged staffs in their hands, and, springing from the ground, they waved their arms around their heads, and sent forth the most hideous yells.

At dinner-time we landed among a party of Fuegians. At first they were not inclined to be friendly, for until the Captain pulled in ahead of the other boats, they kept their slings in their hands. We soon,

In the Strait of Magellan ... the distant channels between the mountains appeared from their gloominess to lead beyond the confines of this world.

We ... doubled the weather-beaten Cape Horn (p. 96)

Tierra del Fuego

We were delighted by seeing the veil of mist gradually rise from Sarmiento, and display it to our view.... Its base, for about an eighth of its total height, is clothed by dusky woods, and above this a field of snow extends to the summit. (p. 112)

Numerous cascades pour their waters through the woods into the narrow channel below. In many parts magnificent glaciers extend from the mountainside to the water's edge. (pp. 107–8)

They may be likened to great frozen Niagaras; and perhaps these cataracts of blue ice are full as beautiful as the moving ones of water. (p. 113)

(Above) ... *a globular, bright-yellow fungus, which grows in vast numbers on the beech-trees. ... With the exception of a few berries ... the natives eat no vegetable food besides this fungus.* (p. 112)

(Right) ... *the Fuegians whom we had on board. ...* (p. 93)

The only garment [of the Fuegians] *consists of a mantle made of guanaco skin, with the wool outside.* (p. 92)

however, delighted them by trifling presents, such as tying red tape round their heads. They liked our biscuit, but one of the savages touched with his finger some of the meat preserved in tin cases which I was eating, and feeling it soft and cold, showed as much disgust at it as I should have done at putrid blubber. Jemmy was thoroughly ashamed of his countrymen, and declared his own tribe were quite different – in which he was woefully mistaken.

It was as easy to please as it was difficult to satisfy these savages. Young and old, men and children, never ceased repeating the word 'yammerschooner', which means 'give me'. After pointing to almost every object one after the other, even to the buttons on our coats, and saying their favourite word in as many intonations as possible, they would then use it in a neuter sense, and vacantly repeat 'yammerschooner'. After yammerschoonering for any article very eagerly, they would by a simple artifice point to their young women or little children, as much as to say, 'If you will not give it me, surely you will to such as these'.

21 JANUARY

At night we endeavoured in vain to find an uninhabited cove; and at last were obliged to bivouac not far from a party of natives. They were very inoffensive as long as they were few in numbers, but in the morning being joined by others they showed symptoms of hostility, and we thought that we should have come to a skirmish. A European labours under great disadvantages when treating with savages like these, who have not the least idea of the power of fire-arms. In the very act of levelling his musket he appears to the savage far inferior to a man armed with a bow and arrow, a spear, or even a sling. Nor is it easy to teach them our superiority except by striking a fatal blow. Like wild beasts, they do not appear to compare numbers; for each individual, if attacked, instead of retiring, will endeavour to dash your brains out with a stone, as certainly as a tiger under similar circumstances would tear you.

Captain FitzRoy on one occasion being very anxious, from good reasons, to frighten away a small party, first flourished a cutlass near them, at which they only laughed. He then twice fired his pistol close to a native. The man both times looked astounded, and carefully but quickly rubbed his head; he then stared awhile, and gabbled to his companions, but he never seemed to think of running away. We can hardly put ourselves in the position of these savages, and understand their actions. In the case of this Fuegian, the possibility of such a sound as the report of a gun close to his ear could never have entered his mind. He perhaps literally did not for a second know whether it was a sound or a blow, and therefore very naturally rubbed his head. In a similar manner, when a savage sees a mark struck by a bullet, it may be some time before he is able at all to understand how it is effected; for the fact of a body being invisible from its velocity would perhaps be to him an idea totally inconceivable. Moreover, the extreme force of a bullet, that penetrates a hard substance without tearing it, may convince the savage that it has no force at all. Certainly I believe that many savages of the lowest grade, such as these of Tierra del Fuego, have seen objects struck, and even small animals killed by the musket, without being in the least aware how deadly an instrument it is ...

23 JANUARY

During the night the news had spread, and early in the morning a fresh party arrived, belonging to the Tekenika, or Jemmy's tribe. Several of them had run so fast that their noses were bleeding, and their mouths frothed from the rapidity with which they talked; and with their naked bodies all bedaubed with black, white, and red, they looked like so many demoniacs who had been fighting. We then proceeded (accompanied by twelve canoes, each holding four or five people) down Ponsonby Sound to the spot where poor Jemmy expected to find his mother and relatives. He had already heard that his father was dead; but as he had had a 'dream in his head' to that effect, he did not seem to care much about it, and repeatedly comforted himself with the very natural reflection, 'Me no help it'. He was not able to learn any particulars regarding his father's death, as his relations would not speak about it.

Jemmy was now in a district well known to him, and guided the boats to a quiet, pretty cove named Woollya, surrounded by islets, every one of which and every point had its proper native name. We found here a family of Jemmy's tribe, but not his relations. We made friends with them, and in the evening they sent a canoe to inform Jemmy's mother and brothers. The cove was bordered by some acres of good sloping land, not covered (as elsewhere) either by peat or by forest-trees. Captain FitzRoy originally intended to have taken York Minster and Fuegia to their own tribe on the west coast; but as they expressed a wish to remain here, and as the spot was singularly favourable, Captain FitzRoy determined to settle here the whole party, including Matthews, the missionary. Five days were spent in building for them three large wigwams, in landing their goods, in digging two gardens, and sowing seeds.

24 JANUARY

The next morning after our arrival (24 January) the Fuegians began to pour in, and Jemmy's mother and brothers arrived. Jemmy recognised the stentorian voice of one of his brothers at a prodigious distance. The meeting was less interesting than that between a horse, turned out into a field, when he joins an old companion. There was no demonstration of affection: they simply stared for a short time at each other, and the mother immediately went to look after her canoe. We heard, however, through York, that the mother had been inconsolable for the loss of Jemmy, and had searched everywhere for him, thinking that he might have been left after having been taken in the boat. The women took much notice of and were very kind to Fuegia. We had already perceived that Jemmy had almost forgotten his own language. I should think there was scarcely another human being with so small a stock of language, for his English was very imperfect. It was laughable, but almost pitiable, to hear him speak to his wild brother in English, and then ask him in Spanish ('No sabe?') whether he did not understand him.

Everything went on peaceably during the three next days, whilst the gardens were digging and wigwams building. We estimated the number of natives at about 120. The women worked hard, whilst the men lounged about all day long, watching us. They asked for everything they saw, and stole what they could. They were delighted at our dancing and singing, and were particularly interested at seeing us wash in a neighbouring brook; they did not pay much attention to anything else, not even to our boats. . . .

Captain FitzRoy, to avoid the chance of an encounter, which would have been fatal to so many of the Fuegians, thought it advisable for us to sleep at a cove a few miles distant. Matthews, with his usual quiet fortitude (remarkable in a man apparently possessing little energy of character), determined to stay with the Fuegians, who evinced no alarm for themselves; and so we left them to pass their first awful night. . . .

29 JANUARY

Early in the morning we arrived at the point where the Beagle Channel divides into two arms, and we entered the northern one. The scenery here becomes even grander than before. The lofty mountains on the north side compose the granitic axis, or backbone of the country, and boldly rise to a height of between three and four thousand feet, with one peak above 6000 feet. They are covered by a wide mantle of perpetual snow, and numerous cascades pour their waters through the woods into the narrow channel below. In many parts magnificent glaciers extend from the mountainside to the water's edge. It is scarcely possible to imagine any thing more beautiful than the beryl-like blue of these glaciers, and especially as contrasted with the dead white of the upper expanse of snow. The fragments which had fallen from the glacier into the water, were floating away, and the channel with its icebergs presented, for the space of a mile, a miniature likeness of the Polar Sea.

The boats being hauled on shore at our dinner-hour, we were admiring from the distance of half a mile a perpendicular cliff of ice, and were wishing that some more fragments would fall. At last, down came a mass with a roaring noise, and immediately we saw the smooth outline of a wave travelling towards us. The men ran down as quickly as they could to the boats, for the chance of their being dashed to pieces was evident. One of the seamen just caught hold of the bows, as the curling breaker reached it: he was knocked over and over, but not hurt, and the boats, though thrice lifted on high and let fall again, received no damage. This was most fortunate for us, for we were a hundred miles distant from the ship, and we should have been left without provisions or fire-arms. . . .

6 FEBRUARY

We arrived at Woollya. Matthews gave so bad an account of the conduct of the Fuegians, that Captain FitzRoy determined to take him back to the *Beagle*, and ultimately he was left at New Zealand, where his brother was a missionary. From the time of our leaving, a regular system of plunder commenced. Fresh parties of the natives kept arriving: York and Jemmy lost many things, and Matthews almost everything which had not been concealed underground. Every article seemed to have been torn up and divided by the natives. Matthews described the watch he was obliged always to keep as most harassing. Night and day he was surrounded by the natives, who tried to tire him out by making an incessant noise close to his head.

One day an old man, whom Matthews asked to leave his wigwam, immediately returned with a large stone in his hand. Another day a whole party came armed with stones and stakes, and some of the younger men and Jemmy's brother were crying: Matthews met them with presents. Another party showed by signs that they wished to strip him naked and pluck all the hairs out of his face and body. I think we arrived just in time to save his life. Jemmy's relatives had been so vain and foolish, that they had showed to strangers their plunder, and their manner of obtaining it.

It was quite melancholy leaving the three Fuegians with their savage countrymen; but it was a great comfort that they had no personal fears. York, being a powerful resolute man, was pretty sure to get on well, together with his wife Fuegia. Poor Jemmy looked rather disconsolate, and would then, I have little doubt, have been glad to have returned with us. His own brother had stolen many things from him; and as he remarked, 'What fashion call that?' He abused his countrymen, 'all bad men, no sabe (know) nothing,' and, though I never heard him swear before, 'damned fools'. Our three Fuegians, though they had been only three years with civilised men, would, I am sure, have been glad to have retained their new habits: but this was obviously impossible. I fear it is more than doubtful, whether their visit will have been of any use to them.

[*At this point the Journal jumps ahead one full year, in order to record the end of FitzRoy's experiment.*]

SECOND VISIT TO TIERRA DEL FUEGO, 28 FEBRUARY TO 5 MARCH 1834

JOURNAL 28 FEBRUARY

The *Beagle* anchored in a beautiful little cove at the eastern entrance of the Beagle Channel. Captain FitzRoy determined on the bold and, as it proved, successful attempt to beat against the westerly winds by the same route which we had followed in the boats to the settlement at Woollya. We did not see many natives until we were near Ponsonby Sound, where we were followed by ten or twelve canoes. The natives did not at all understand the reason of our tacking, and, instead of meeting us at each tack, vainly strove to follow us in our zig-zag course. I was amused at finding what a difference the circumstance of being quite superior in force made, in the interest of beholding these savages. While in the boats I got to hate the very sound of their voices, so much trouble did they give us. The first and last word was 'yammerschooner'.... But now, the more Fuegians the merrier; and very merry work it was. Both parties laughing, wondering, gaping at each other; we pitying them for giving us good fish and crabs for rags, etc., they grasping at the chance of finding people so foolish as to exchange such splendid ornaments for a good supper. It was most amusing to see the undisguised smile of satisfaction with which one young woman with her face painted black, tied several bits of scarlet cloth round her head with rushes. Her husband, who enjoyed the very universal privilege in this country of possessing two wives, evidently became jealous of all the attention paid to his young wife;

and, after a consultation with his naked beauties, was paddled away by them.

Some of the Fuegians plainly showed that they had a fair notion of barter. I gave one man a large nail (a most valuable present) without making any signs for a return; but he immediately picked out two fish, and handed them up on the point of his spear. If any present was designed for one canoe, and it fell near another, it was invariably given to the right owner. . . .

On 5 March we anchored in the cove at Woollya, but we saw not a soul there. We were alarmed at this, for the natives in Ponsonby Sound showed by gestures, that there had been fighting; and we afterwards heard that the dreaded Oens men had made a descent. Soon a canoe, with a little flag flying, was seen approaching, with one of the men in it washing the paint off his face. This man was poor Jemmy – now a thin, haggard savage with long disordered hair, and naked, except [for] a bit of a blanket round his waist. We did not recognise him till he was close to us; for he was ashamed of himself, and turned his back to the ship. We had left him plump, fat, clean, and well dressed: I never saw so complete and grievous a change.

As soon however as he was clothed, and the first flurry was over, things wore a good appearance. He dined with Captain FitzRoy, and ate his dinner as tidily as formerly. He told us he had 'too much' (meaning enough) to eat, that he was not cold, that his relations were very good people, and that he did not wish to go back to England. In the evening we found out the cause of this great change in Jemmy's feelings, in the arrival of his young and nice-looking wife. With his usual good feeling, he brought two beautiful otter-skins for two of his best friends, and some spearheads and arrows made with his own hands for the Captain. He said he had built a canoe for himself, and he boasted that he could talk a little of his own language! But it is a most singular fact, that he appears to have taught all his tribe some English: an old man spontaneously announced 'Jemmy Button's wife'. Jemmy had lost all his property. He told us that York Minster had built a large canoe, and with his wife Fuegia, had several months since gone to his own country, and had taken farewell by an act of consummate villainy; he persuaded Jemmy and his mother to come with him, and then on the way deserted them by night, stealing every article of their property.

Jemmy went to sleep on shore, and in the morning returned, and remained on board till the ship got under weigh, which frightened his wife, who continued crying violently till he got into his canoe.

He returned loaded with valuable property. Every soul on board was heartily sorry to shake hands with him for the last time. I do not now doubt that he will be as happy as, perhaps happier than, if he had never left his own country. Every one must sincerely hope that Captain FitzRoy's noble hope may be fulfilled, of being rewarded for the many generous sacrifices which he made for these Fuegians, by some shipwrecked sailor being protected by the descendants of Jemmy Button and his tribe! When Jemmy reached the shore, he lighted a signal fire, and the smoke curled up, bidding us a last and long farewell, as the ship stood on her course into the open sea.

The perfect equality among the individuals composing the Fuegian tribes, must for a long time retard their civilisation. As we see those animals, whose instinct compels them to live in society and obey a chief, are most capable of improvement, so is it with the races of mankind. Whether we look at it as a cause or a consequence, the more civilised always have the most artificial governments.... In Tierra del Fuego, until some chief shall arise with power sufficient to secure any acquired advantage, such as the domesticated animals, it seems scarcely possible that the political state of the country can be improved. At present, even a piece of cloth given to one is torn into shreds and distributed, and no one individual becomes richer than another. On the other hand, it is difficult to understand how a chief can arise till there is property of some sort by which he might manifest his superiority and increase his power.

I believe, in this extreme part of South America, man exists in a lower state of improvement than in any other part of the world. The South Sea Islanders of the two races inhabiting the Pacific, are comparatively civilised. The Eskimo in his subterranean hut enjoys some of the comforts of life, and in his canoe, when fully equipped, manifests much skill. Some of the tribes of Southern Africa, prowling about in search of roots, and living concealed on the wild and arid plains, are sufficiently wretched. The Australian, in the simplicity of the arts of life, comes nearest the Fuegian: he can, however, boast of his boomerang, his spear and throwing-stick, his method of climbing trees, of tracking animals, and of hunting. Although the Australian may be superior in acquirements, it by no means follows that he is likewise superior in mental capacity: indeed, from what I saw of the Fuegians when on board, and from what I have read of the Australians, I should think the case was exactly the reverse....

There is one vegetable production deserving notice from its importance as an article of food to the Fuegians. It is a globular, bright-yellow fungus,which grows in vast numbers on the beech-trees. When young it is elastic and turgid, with a smooth surface; but when mature, it shrinks, becomes tougher, and has its entire surface deeply pitted or honeycombed. This fungus belongs to a new and curious genus; I found a second species on another species of beech in Chile; and Dr Hooker informs me, that just lately a third species had been discovered on a third species of beech in Van Diemen's Land. How singular is this relationship between parasitical fungi and the trees on which they grow in distant parts of the world! In Tierra del Fuego the fungus in its tough and mature state is collected in large quantities by the women and children, and is eaten uncooked. It has a mucilaginous, slightly sweet taste, with a faint smell like that of a mushroom. With the exception of a few berries, chiefly of a dwarf arbutus, the natives eat no vegetable food besides this fungus. In New Zealand, before the introduction of the potato, the roots of the fern were largely consumed; at the present time, I believe, Tierra del Fuego is the only country in the world where a cryptogamic plant affords a staple article of food.

TIERRA DEL FUEGO: THE LAST VIEW, 8–10 JUNE 1834

8 JUNE

We weighed anchor early in the morning and left Port Famine. Captain FitzRoy determined to leave the Strait of Magellan by the Magdalen Channel, which had not long been discovered. Our course lay due south, down that gloomy passage which I have before alluded to, as appearing to lead to another and worse world. The wind was fair, but the atmosphere was very thick; so that we missed much curious scenery. The dark ragged clouds were rapidly driven over the mountains, from their summits nearly down to their bases. The glimpses which we caught through the dusky mass, were highly interesting; jagged points, cones of snow, blue glaciers, strong outlines, marked on a lurid sky, were seen at different distances and heights. In the midst of such scenery we anchored at Cape Turn, close to Mount Sarmiento, which was then hidden in the clouds. At the base of the lofty and almost perpendicular sides of our little cove there was one deserted wigwam, and it alone reminded us that man sometimes wandered into these desolate regions. But it would be difficult to imagine a scene where he seemed to have fewer claims or less authority. The inanimate works of nature – rock, ice, snow, wind, and water, all warring with each other, yet combined against man – here reigned in absolute sovereignty.

In the morning we were delighted by seeing the veil of mist gradually rise from Sarmiento, and display it to our view. This mountain, which is one of the highest in Tierra del Fuego, has an altitude of 6800 feet. Its base, for about an eighth of its total height, is clothed by dusky woods, and above this a field of snow extends to the summit. These vast piles of snow, which never melt, and seem destined to last as long as the world holds together, present a noble and even sublime spectacle. The outline of the mountain was admirably clear and defined. Owing to the abundance of light reflected from the white and glittering surface, no shadows were cast on any part; and those lines which intersected the sky could alone be distinguished: hence the mass stood out in in the boldest relief. Several glaciers descended in a winding course from the upper great expanse of snow to the sea-coast: they may be likened to great frozen Niagaras; and perhaps these cataracts of blue ice are full as beautiful as the moving ones of water. . . .

10 JUNE

The descent of glaciers to the sea must, I conceive, mainly depend (subject, of course, to a proper supply of snow in the upper region) on the lowness of the line of perpetual snow on steep mountains near the coast. As the snow-line is so low in Tierra del Fuego, we might have expected that many of the glaciers would have reached the sea. Nevertheless I was astonished when I first saw a range, only from 3000 to 4000 feet in height, in the latitude of Cumberland, with every valley filled with streams of ice descending to the sea-coast. Almost every arm of the sea, which penetrates to the interior higher chain, not only in Tierra del Fuego, but on the coast for 650 miles north-wards, is terminated by 'tremendous and astonishing glaciers', as described by one of the officers on the survey.

Great masses of ice frequently fall from these icy cliffs, and the crash reverberates like the broadside of a man-of-war, through the lonely channels. These falls, as noticed above [p. 108], produce great waves which break on the adjoining coasts. It is known that earthquakes frequently cause masses of earth to fall from seacliffs: how terrific, then, would be the effect of a severe shock (and such occur here) on a body like a glacier, already in motion, and traversed by fissures! I can readily believe that the water would be fairly beaten back out of the deepest channel, and then, returning with an over-whelming force, would whirl about huge masses of rock like so much chaff. . . . One sight of such a coast is enough to make a landsman dream for a week about shipwrecks, peril, and death; and with this sight we bade farewell for ever to Tierra del Fuego.

[*The* Beagle *then sailed northwards up the Pacific coast of South America towards Valparaiso, by way of Chiloe.*]

Chile

JOURNAL 23 JULY 1834

The *Beagle* anchored late at night in the bay of Valparaiso, the chief seaport of Chile. When morning came, everything appeared delightful. After Tierra del Fuego, the climate felt quite delicious – the atmosphere so dry, and the heavens so clear and blue, with the sun shining brightly, that all nature seemed sparkling with life. The view from the anchorage is very pretty. The town is built at the very foot of a range of hills, about 1600 feet high, and rather steep. From its position it consists of one long, straggling street which runs parallel to the beach and, wherever a ravine comes down, the houses are piled up on each side of it. The rounded hills, being only partially protected by a very scanty vegetation, are worn into numberless little gullies, which expose a singularly bright red soil. From this cause, and from the low whitewashed houses with tiled roofs, the view reminded me of Santa Cruz in Tenerife.

In a north-easterly direction there are some fine glimpses of the Andes, but these mountains appear much grander when viewed from the neighbouring hills: the great distance at which they are situated, can then more readily be perceived. The volcano of Aconcagua is particularly magnificent. This huge and irregularly conical mass has an elevation greater than that of Chimborazo, for, from measurements made by the officers in the *Beagle*, its height is no less than 23,000 feet. The Cordillera, however, viewed from this point, owe the greater part of their beauty to the atmosphere through which they are seen. When the sun was setting in the Pacific, it was admirable to watch how clearly their rugged outlines could be distinguished, yet how varied and how delicate were the shades of their colour.

I had the good fortune to find living here Mr Richard Corfield, an old schoolfellow and friend, to whose hospitality and kindness I was greatly indebted, in having afforded me a most pleasant residence during the *Beagle*'s stay in Chile. The immediate neighbourhood of Valparaiso is not very productive to the naturalist. During the long summer the wind blows steadily from the southward, and a little off shore, so that rain never falls; during the three winter months, however, it is sufficiently abundant. The vegetation in consequence is very scanty. Except in some deep valleys, there are no trees, and only a little grass and a few low bushes are scattered over the less steep parts of the hills. When we reflect that at the distance of 350 miles to the south, this side of the Andes is completely hidden by one impenetrable forest, the contrast is very remarkable....

14 AUGUST

I set out on a riding excursion, for the purpose of geologising the basal parts of the Andes, which alone at this time of the year are not shut up by the winter snow. Our first day's ride was northward along the sea-coast. After dark we reached the hacienda of Quintero, the estate which formerly belonged to Lord Cochrane. My object in coming here was to see the great beds of shells, which stand some yards above the level of the sea, and are burnt for lime. The proofs of the elevation of this whole line of coast are unequivocal: at the height of a few hundred feet old-looking shells are numerous, and I found some at 1300 feet. These shells either lie loose on the surface, or are embedded in a reddish-black vegetable mould. I was much surprised to find under the microscope that this vegetable mould is really marine mud, full of minute particles of organic bodies....

DIARY 5 AUGUST

It seems not a very improbable conjecture that the want of animals may be owing to none having been created since this country was raised from the sea.

JOURNAL 16 AUGUST

The major-domo of the hacienda was good enough to give me a guide and fresh horses and in the morning we set out to ascend the Campana, or Bell Mountain, which is 6400 feet high. The paths were very bad, but both the geology and scenery amply repaid the trouble. We reached, by the evening, a spring called the Agua del Guanaco, which is situated at a great height....

We unsaddled our horses near the spring, and prepared to pass the night. The evening was fine, and the atmosphere so clear that the masts of the vessels at anchor in the bay of Valparaiso, although no less than twenty-six geographical miles distant, could be distinguished clearly as little black streaks. A ship doubling the point under sail, appeared as a bright white speck. Anson expresses much surprise, in his voyage, at the distance at which his vessels were discovered from the coast; but he did not sufficiently allow for the height of the land, and the great transparency of the air.

The setting of the sun was glorious; the valleys being black, whilst the snowy peaks of the Andes yet retained a ruby tint. When it was dark, we made a fire beneath a little arbour of bamboos, fried our charqui (or dried slips of beef), took our maté, and were quite comfortable. There is an inexpressible charm in thus living in the open air. The evening was calm and still. The shrill noise of the mountain bizcacha, and the faint cry of a goatsucker, were occasionally to be heard. Besides these, few birds, or even insects, frequent these dry, parched mountains.

17 AUGUST

In the morning we climbed up the rough mass of greenstone which crowns the summit. This rock, as frequently happens, was much shattered and broken into huge angular fragments. I observed, however, one remarkable circumstance, namely, that many of the surfaces presented every degree of freshness – some appearing as if broken the day before – whilst on others lichens had either just become, or had long grown, attached. I so fully believed that this was owing to the frequent earthquakes, that I felt inclined to hurry from below each loose pile. As one might very easily be deceived in a fact of this kind I doubted its accuracy, until ascending Mount Wellington in Van Diemen's Land, where earthquakes do not occur; and there I saw the summit of the mountain similarly composed and similarly shattered, but all the blocks appeared as if they had been hurled into their present position thousands of years ago.

We spent the day on the summit, and I never enjoyed one more thoroughly. Chile, bounded by the Andes and the Pacific, was seen as in a map. The pleasure from the scenery, in itself beautiful, was heightened by the many reflections which arose from the mere view of the Campana range with its lesser parallel ones, and of the broad valley of Quillota directly intersecting them. Who can avoid wondering at the force which has upheaved these mountains, and even more so at the countless ages which it must have required, to have broken through, removed, and levelled whole masses of them? It is well in this case to call to mind the vast shingle and sedimentary beds of Patagonia, which, if heaped on the Cordillera, would increase its height by so many thousand feet. When in that country I wondered how any mountain-chain could have supplied such masses, and not have been utterly obliterated. We must not now reverse the wonder, and doubt whether all-powerful time can grind down mountains – even the gigantic Cordillera – into gravel and mud.

The appearance of the Andes was different from that which I had expected. The lower line of the snow was of course horizontal, and to this line the even summits of the range seemed quite parallel. Only at long intervals, a group of points or a single cone, showed where a volcano had existed, or does now exist. Hence the range resembled a great solid wall, surmounted here and there by a tower, and making a most perfect barrier to the country.

Almost every part of the hill had been drilled by attempts to open gold-mines: the rage for mining has left scarcely a spot in Chile unexamined. I spent the evening as before, talking round the fire with my two companions. The guasos of Chile, who correspond to the gauchos of the Pampas, are, however, a very different set of beings. Chile is the more civilised of the two countries, and the inhabitants, in consequence, have lost much individual character. Gradations in rank are much more strongly marked: the guaso does not by any means consider every man his equal; and I was quite surprised to find that my companions did not like to eat at the same time with myself. This feeling of inequality is a necessary consequence of the existence of an aristocracy of wealth. It is said that some few of the greater landowners possess from five to ten thousand pounds sterling per annum: an inequality of riches which I believe is not met with in any of the cattle-breeding countries eastward of the Andes. A traveller does not here meet that unbounded hospitality which refuses all payment, but yet is so kindly offered that no scruples can be raised in accepting it. Almost every house in Chile will receive you for the night, but a trifle is expected to be given in the morning: even a rich man will accept two or three shillings. The gaucho, although he may be a cut-throat, is a gentleman; the guaso is in few respects better, but at the same time a vulgar, ordinary fellow. The two men, although employed much in the same manner, are different in their habits and attire, and the peculiarities of each are universal in their respective countries. The gaucho seems part of his horse, and scorns to exert himself excepting when on its back; the guaso may be hired to work as a labourer in the fields. The former lives entirely on animal food; the latter almost wholly on vegetable. We do not here see the white boots, the broad drawers, and scarlet chilipa, the picturesque costume of the pampas. Here, common trousers are protected by black and green worsted leggings. The poncho, however, is common to both. The chief pride of the guaso lies in his spurs; which are absurdly large. I measured one which was six inches in the *diameter* of the rowel, and the rowel itself contained upwards of thirty points. . . .

During the day I felt very unwell.

Our course was now directed towards Valparaiso, which with great difficulty I reached on the 27th, and was there confined to my bed till the end of October. During this time I was an inmate in Mr Corfield's house, whose kindness to me I do not know how to express.

I will here add a few observations on some of the animals and birds of Chile. The puma, or South American lion, is not uncommon. This animal has a wide geographical range; being found from the equatorial forests, throughout the deserts of Patagonia, as far south as the damp and cold latitudes (53° to 54°) of Tierra del Fuego. I have seen its footsteps in the Cordillera of central Chile, at an elevation of at least 10,000 feet. In La Plata the puma preys chiefly on deer, ostriches, bizcacha, and other small quadrupeds; it there seldom attacks cattle or horses, and most rarely man. In Chile, however, it destroys many young horses and cattle, owing probably to the scarcity of other quadrupeds. I heard, likewise, of two men and a woman who had been thus killed. . . . The puma is described as being very crafty: when pursued, it often returns on its former track, and then suddenly making a spring on one side, waits there till the dogs have passed by. It is a very silent animal, uttering no cry even when wounded, and only rarely during the breeding season.

The puma, after eating its fill, covers the carcass with many large bushes, and lies down to watch it. This habit is often the cause of its being discovered; for the condors wheeling in the air every now and then descend to partake of the feast, and, being angrily driven away, rise all together on the wing. The Chileno guaso then knows there is a lion watching his prey. The word is given – and men and dogs hurry to the chase.

Two species of humming-birds are common. Trochilus forficatus is found over a space of 2500 miles on the west coast, from the hot dry country of Lima, to the forests of Tierra del Fuego – where it may be seen flitting about in snow-storms. In the wooded island of Chiloe, which has an extremely humid climate, this little bird, skipping from side to side amidst the dripping foliage, is perhaps more abundant than almost any other kind. I opened the stomachs of several specimens, shot in different parts of the continent, and in all remains of insects were as numerous as in the stomach of a creeper. When this species migrates in the summer southward, it is replaced by the arrival of another species coming from the north. This second kind (Trochilus gigas) is a very large bird for the delicate family to which it belongs. When on the wing its appearance is singular. Like others of the genus, it moves from place to place with a rapidity which may be compared to that of syrphus amongst flies, and sphinx among moths; but whilst hovering over a flower, it flaps its wings with a very slow and powerful movement, totally different from that vibratory one common to most of the species, which produces the humming noise. I never saw any other bird, where the force of its wings appeared (as in a butterfly) so powerful in proportion to the weight of its body. When hovering by a flower, its tail is constantly expanded and shut like a fan, the body being kept in a nearly vertical position. This action appears to steady and support the bird, between the slow movements of its wings. Although flying from flower to flower in search of food, its stomach generally contained abundant remains of insects, which I suspect are much more the object of its search than honey. The note of this species, like that of nearly the whole family, is extremely shrill.

[*The early weeks of 1835 were spent by the* Beagle *surveying the southern coast of Chile in the region of Chiloe and the Chonos archipelago. In February of that year she returned to Valdivia.*]

EARTHQUAKE IN VALDIVIA, 20 FEBRUARY TO 7 MARCH 1835

JOURNAL 20 FEBRUARY

This day has been memorable in the annals of Valdivia for the most severe earthquake experienced by the oldest inhabitant. I happened to be on shore, and was lying down in the wood to rest myself. It came on suddenly, and lasted two minutes, but the time appeared much longer. The rocking of the ground was very sensible. The undulations appeared to my companion and myself to come from due east, whilst others thought they proceeded from south-west: this shows how difficult it sometimes is to perceive the direction of the vibrations. There was no difficulty in standing upright, but the motion made me almost giddy: it was something like the movement of a vessel in a little cross-ripple, or still more like that felt by a person skating over thin ice, which bends under the weight of his body.

A bad earthquake at once destroys our oldest associations: the earth, the very emblem of solidity, has moved beneath our feet like a thin crust over a fluid. One second of time has created in the mind a strange idea of insecurity, which hours of reflection would not have produced. In the forest, as a breeze moved the trees, I felt only the earth tremble, but saw no other effect. Captain FitzRoy and some officers were at the town during the shock, and there the scene was more striking, for although the houses, from being built of wood, did not fall, they were violently shaken, and the boards creaked and rattled together. The people rushed out of doors in the greatest alarm.

It is these accompaniments that create the perfect horror of earthquakes, experienced by all who have thus seen, as well as felt, their effects. Within the forest it was a deeply interesting, but by no means an awe-inspiring phenomenon. The tides were very curiously affected. The great shock took place at the time of low water; and an old woman who was on the beach told me, that the water flowed very quickly, but not in great waves, to high-water mark, and then as quickly returned to its proper level; this was also evident by the line of wet sand. . . .

5 MARCH
I landed at Talcahuano, and afterwards rode to Concepción. Both towns presented the most awful yet interesting spectacle I ever beheld. To a person who had formerly known them it possibly might have been still more impressive, for the ruins were so mingled together, and the whole scene possessed so little the air of a habitable place, that it was scarcely possible to imagine its former condition. The earthquake commenced at half past eleven o'clock in the forenoon. If it had happened in the middle of the night, the greater number of the inhabitants (which in this one province amount to many thousands) must have perished, instead of less than a hundred: as it was, the invariable practice of running out of doors at the first trembling of the ground, alone saved them. . . .

The mayor-domo at Quiriquina told me that the first notice he received of it was finding both the horse he rode, and himself, rolling together on the ground. Rising up, he was again thrown down. He also told me that some cows which were standing on the steep side of the island were rolled into the sea. The great wave caused the destruction of many cattle: on one low island near the head of the bay seventy animals were washed off and drowned. It is generally thought that this has been the worst earthquake ever recorded in Chile; but as the very severe ones occur only after long intervals this cannot easily be known – nor indeed would a much worse shock have made any great difference, for the ruin was now complete. Innumerable small tremblings followed the great earthquake, and within the first twelve days no less than three hundred were counted.

After viewing Concepción, I cannot understand how the greater number of inhabitants escaped unhurt. The houses in many parts fell outwards, thus forming in the middle of the streets little hillocks of brickwork and rubbish.

As shock succeeded shock at the interval of a few minutes, no one dared approach the shattered ruins; and no one knew whether his dearest friends and relations were not perishing from the want of help. Those who had saved any property were obliged to keep a constant watch, for thieves prowled about, and at each little trembling of the ground, with one hand they beat their breasts and cried 'misericordia!' and then with the other filched what they could from the ruins. The thatched roofs fell over the fires, and flames burst forth in all parts. Hundreds knew themselves ruined, and few had the means of providing food for the day.

Earthquakes alone are sufficient to destroy the prosperity of any country. If beneath England the now inert subterranean forces should exert those powers, which most assuredly in former geological ages they have exerted, how completely would the entire condition of the country be changed! What would become of the lofty houses, thickly-packed cities, great manufactories, the beautiful public and private edifices? If the new period of disturbance were first to commence by some great earthquake in the dead of the night, how terrific would be the carnage! England would at once be bankrupt; all papers, records, and accounts would from that moment be lost. Government being unable to collect the taxes and failing to maintain its authority, the hand of violence and rapine would remain uncontrolled. In every large town famine would go forth, pestilence and death following in its train.

Shortly after the shock, a great wave was seen from the distance of three or four miles, approaching in the middle of the bay with a smooth outline; but along the shore it tore up cottages and trees, as it swept onwards with irresistible force. At the head of the bay it broke in a fearful line of white breakers, which rushed up to a height of twenty-three vertical feet above the highest spring tides. Their force must have been prodigious; for at the fort a cannon with its carriage, estimated at four tons in weight, was moved fifteen feet inwards. A schooner was left in the midst of the ruins, 200 yards from the beach....

One old woman with a little boy, four or five years old, ran into a boat, but there was nobody to row it out: the boat was consequently dashed against an anchor and cut in twain. The old woman was drowned, but the child was picked up some hours afterwards clinging to the wreck. Pools of salt water were still standing amidst the ruins of the houses, and children, making boats with old tables and chairs, appeared as happy as their parents were miserable. It was, however, exceedingly interesting to observe, how much more active and cheerful all appeared than could have been expected. It was remarked with much truth, that from the destruction being universal, no one individual was humbled more than another, or could suspect his friends of coldness – that most grievous result of the loss of wealth. . . .

The most remarkable effect of this earthquake was the permanent elevation of the land: it would probably be far more correct to speak of it as the cause. There can be no doubt that the land round the Bay of Concepción was upraised two or three feet, but it deserves notice that, owing to the wave having obliterated the old lines of tidal action on the sloping sandy shores, I could discover no evidence of this fact, except in the united testimony of the inhabitants, that one little rocky shoal, now exposed, was formerly covered with water. At the island of Santa Maria (about thirty miles distant) the elevation was greater: on one part, Captain FitzRoy found beds of putrid mussel-shells *still adhering to the rocks* ten feet above high-water mark: the inhabitants had formerly dived at low-water spring-tides for these shells. The elevation of this province is particularly interesting, from its having been the theatre of several other violent earthquakes, and from the vast numbers of sea-shells scattered over the land, up to a height of certainly 600, and I believe, of 1000 feet. At Valparaiso, as I have remarked, similar shells are found at the height of 1300 feet: it is hardly possible to doubt that this great elevation has been effected by successive small uprisings, such as that which accompanied or caused the earthquake of this year, and likewise by an insensibly slow rise, which is certainly in progress on some parts of this coast. . . .

The space, from under which volcanic matter on the 20th was actually erupted, is 720 miles in one line, and 400 miles in another line at right angles to the first: hence, in all probability, a subterranean lake of lava is here stretched out of nearly double the area of the Black Sea. From the intimate and complicated manner in which the elevatory and eruptive forces were shown to be connected during this train of phenomena, we may confidently come to the conclusion that the forces which slowly and by little starts uplift continents, and those which at successive periods pour forth volcanic matter from open orifices, are identical. From many reasons, I believe that the frequent quakings of the earth on this line of coast, are caused by the rending of the strata, necessarily consequent on the tension of the land when upraised, and their injection by fluidified rock.

OVER THE ANDES TO MENDOZA, 11 MARCH TO 10 APRIL 1835

11 MARCH

We anchored at Valparaiso, and two days afterwards I set out to cross the Cordillera.... In this part of Chile there are two passes across the Andes to Mendoza: the one most commonly used – namely, that of Aconcagua or Uspallata – is situated some way to the north; the other, called the Portillo, is to the south, and nearer, but more lofty and dangerous.

18 MARCH

We set out for the Portillo pass. Leaving Santiago we crossed the wide, burnt-up plain on which that city stands, and in the afternoon arrived at the Maypu, one of the principal rivers in Chile.... At night we slept at a cottage. Our manner of travelling was delightfully independent. In the inhabited parts we bought a little firewood, hired pasture for the animals, and bivouacked in the corner of the same field with them. Carrying an iron pot, we cooked and ate our supper under a cloudless sky, and knew no trouble. My companions were Mariano Gonzales, who had formerly accompanied me in Chile, and an 'arriero', with his ten mules and a 'madrina'. The madrina (or godmother) is a most important personage: she is an old steady mare, with a little bell round her neck, and wherever she goes, the mules, like good children, follow her. The affection of these animals for their madrinas saves infinite trouble....

In a troop each animal carries, on a level road, a cargo weighing 416 pounds (more than twenty-nine stone), but in a mountainous country 100 pounds less; yet with what delicate, slim limbs, without any proportional bulk of muscle, these animals support so great a burden! The mule always appears to me a most surprising animal. That a hybrid should possess more reason, memory, obstinacy, social affection, powers of muscular endurance and length of life than either of its parents seems to indicate that art has here outdone nature....

All the main valleys in the Cordillera are characterised by having, on both sides, a fringe or terrace of shingle and sand, rudely stratified, and generally of considerable thickness.... No one fact in the geology

The puma is described as being very crafty. . . . It is a very silent animal, uttering no cry even when wounded, and only rarely during the breeding season. (p. 119)

PANTHERA CONCOLOR

TRIATOMA INFESTANS

... the Benchuca, a species of Reduvius, the great black bug of the Pampas ... It is most disgusting to feel soft wingless insects, about an inch long, crawling over one's body. Before sucking they are quite thin, but afterwards they become round and bloated with blood. (p. 132)

The rivers which flow in these valleys ought rather to be called mountain-torrents. Their inclination is very great, and their water the colour of mud. (p. 129)

of South America interested me more than these terraces of rudely-stratified shingle. They precisely resemble in composition the matter which the torrents in each valley would deposit if they were checked in their course by any cause, such as entering a lake or arm of the sea; but the torrents, instead of depositing matter, are now steadily at work wearing away both the solid rock and these alluvial deposits, along the whole line of every main valley and side valley.

It is impossible here to give the reasons, but I am convinced that the shingle terraces were accumulated, during the gradual elevation of the Cordillera, by the torrents delivering, at successive levels, their detritus on the beach-heads of long narrow arms of the sea, first high up the valleys, then lower and lower down as the land slowly rose. If this be so, and I cannot doubt it, the grand and broken chain of the Cordillera, instead of having been suddenly thrown up, as was till lately the universal, and still is the common opinion of geologists, has been slowly upheaved in mass, in the same gradual manner as the coasts of the Atlantic and Pacific have risen within the recent period. A multitude of facts in the structure of the Cordillera, on this view receive a simple explanation.

The rivers which flow in these valleys ought rather to be called mountain-torrents. Their inclination is very great, and their water the colour of mud. The roar which the Maypu made as it rushed over the great rounded fragments was like that of the sea. Amidst the din of rushing waters, the noise from the stones as they rattled one over another was most distinctly audible even from a distance. This rattling noise, night and day, may be heard along the whole course of the torrent. The sound spoke eloquently to the geologist: the thousands and thousands of stones, which, striking against each other, made the one dull uniform sound, were all hurrying in one direction. It was like thinking on time, where the minute that now glides past is irrecoverable. So was it with these stones. The ocean is their eternity, and each note of that wild music told of one more step towards their destiny.

It is not possible for the mind to comprehend, except by a slow process, any effect which is produced by a cause repeated so often, that the multiplier itself conveys an idea not more definite than the savage implies when he points to the hairs of his head. As often as I have seen beds of mud, sand and shingle accumulated to the thickness of many thousand feet, I have felt inclined to exclaim that causes, such as the present rivers and the present beaches, could never have ground down and produced such masses. But on the other hand, when listening to the rattling noise of these torrents, and calling to mind that whole races of animals have passed away from the face of the earth, and that during this whole period, night and day, these stones have gone rattling onwards in their course, I have thought to myself, can any mountains, any continent, withstand such waste? ...

It is an old story, but not the less wonderful, to hear of shells which were once crawling on the bottom of the sea, now standing nearly 14,000 feet above its level.... The shells in the Peuquenes or oldest ridge, prove ... that it has been upraised 14,000 feet since a Secondary period, which in Europe we are accustomed to consider as far from ancient; but since these shells lived in a moderately deep sea, it can be shown that the area now occupied by the Cordillera, must have subsided several thousand feet – in northern Chile as much as 6000 feet – so as to have allowed that amount of submarine strata to have been heaped on the bed on which the shells lived. The proof is the same with that by which it was shown, that at a much later period since the tertiary shells of Patagonia lived, there must have been there a subsidence of several hundred feet, as well as an ensuing elevation. Daily it is forced home on the mind of the geologist, that nothing, not even the wind that blows, is so unstable as the level of the crust of this earth. ...

About noon we began the tedious ascent of the Peuquenes ridge, and then for the first time experienced some little difficulty in our respiration. The mules would halt every fifty yards, and after resting for a few seconds the poor willing animals started of their own accord again. The short breathing from the rarefied atmosphere is called by the Chilenos 'puna' and they have most ridiculous notions concerning its origin. Some say, 'all the waters here have puna'; others that 'where there is snow there is puna'; – and this no doubt is true. The only sensation I experienced was a slight tightness across the head and chest, like that felt on leaving a warm room and running quickly in frosty weather. There was some imagination even in this, for upon finding fossil shells on the highest ridge I entirely forgot the puna in my delight. Certainly the exertion of walking was extremely great, and the respiration became deep and laborious: I am told that in Potosi (about 13,000 feet above the sea) strangers do not become thoroughly accustomed to the atmosphere for an entire year. The inhabitants all recommend onions for the puna. As this vegetable has sometimes been given in Europe for pectoral complaints, it may possibly be of real service – for my part I found nothing so good as the fossil shells! ...

When near the summit, the wind, as generally happens, was impetuous and extremely cold. On each side of the ridge we had to pass over broad bands of perpetual snow, which were now soon to be covered by a fresh layer. When we reached the crest and looked backwards, a glorious view was presented. The atmosphere resplendently clear, the sky an intense blue, the profound valleys, the wild broken forms, the heaps of ruins, piled up during the lapse of ages, the bright-coloured rocks, contrasted with the quiet mountains of snow; all these together produced a scene no one could have imagined. Neither plant nor bird, excepting a few condors wheeling around the higher pinnacles, distracted my attention from the inanimate mass. I felt glad that I was alone: it was like watching a thunderstorm, or hearing in full orchestra a chorus of the Messiah....

At the place where we slept water necessarily boiled, from the diminished pressure of the atmosphere, at a lower temperature than it does in a less lofty country; the case being the converse of that of a Papin's digester [an early pressure-cooker]. Hence the potatoes, after remaining for some hours in the boiling water, were nearly as hard as ever. The pot was left on the fire all night, and next morning it was boiled again, but yet the potatoes were not cooked. I found out this, by overhearing my two companions discussing the cause; they had come to the simple conclusion that 'the cursed pot (which was a new one) did not choose to boil potatoes'....

23 MARCH
The descent on the eastern side of the Cordillera is much shorter or steeper than on the Pacific side; in other words, the mountains rise more abruptly from the plains than from the alpine country of Chile....

I was much struck with the marked difference between the vegetation of these eastern valleys and those on the Chilean side: yet the climate, as well as the kind of soil, is nearly the same, and the difference of longitude very trifling. The same remark holds good with the quadrupeds, and in a lesser degree with the birds and insects. I may instance the mice, of which I obtained thirteen species on the shores of the Atlantic, and five on the Pacific, and not one of them is identical....

This fact is in perfect accordance with the geological history of the Andes, for these mountains have existed as a great barrier, since the present races of animals have appeared; and therefore, unless we suppose the same species to have been created in two different places, we ought not to expect any closer similarity between the organic beings on the opposite sides of the Andes, than on the opposite shores of the ocean. In both cases, we must leave out of the question those kinds which have been able to cross the barrier, whether of solid rock or salt-water....

25 MARCH

At night I experienced an attack (for it deserves no less a name) of the benchuca, a species of reduvius, the great black bug of the pampas. It is most disgusting to feel soft wingless insects, about an inch long, crawling over one's body. Before sucking they are quite thin, but afterwards they become round and bloated with blood, and in this state are easily crushed. One which I caught at Iquique (for they are found in Chile and Peru), was very empty. When placed on a table, and though surrounded by people, if a finger was presented, the bold insect would immediately protrude its sucker, make a charge, and if allowed, draw blood. No pain was caused by the wound. It was curious to watch its body during the act of sucking, as in less than ten minutes it changed from being as flat as a wafer to a globular form. This one feast, for which the benchuca was indebted to one of the officers, kept it fat during four whole months; but, after the first fortnight, it was quite ready to have another suck.

27 MARCH

We rode on to Mendoza. The country was beautifully cultivated, and resembled Chile. This neighbourhood is celebrated for its fruit; and certainly nothing could appear more flourishing than the vineyards and the orchards of figs, peaches, and olives. We bought watermelons nearly twice as large as a man's head, most deliciously cool and well-flavoured, for a halfpenny apiece; and for the value of threepence, half a wheelbarrowful of peaches....

29 MARCH

We set out on our return to Chile, by the Uspallata Pass situated north of Mendoza. We had to cross a long and most sterile traversia of fifteen leagues. The soil in parts was absolutely bare, in others covered by numberless dwarf cacti, armed with formidable spines, and called by the inhabitants 'little lions'....

30 MARCH

In the central part of the range, at an elevation of about seven thousand feet, I observed on a bare slope some snow-white projecting columns. These were petrified trees, eleven being silicified, and from thirty to forty converted into coarsely-crystallised white calcareous spar. They were abruptly broken off, the upright stumps projecting a few feet above the ground. The trunks measured from three to five feet each in circumference. They stood a little way apart from each other, but the whole formed one group. . . .

It required little geological practice to interpret the marvellous story which this scene at once unfolded, though I confess I was at first so much astonished, that I could scarcely believe the plainest evidence. I saw the spot where a cluster of fine trees once waved their branches on the shores of the Atlantic, when that ocean (now driven back 700 miles) came to the foot of the Andes. I saw that they had sprung from a volcanic soil which has been raised above the level of the sea, and that subsequently this dry land, with its upright trees, had been let down into the depths of the ocean. . . . The ocean which received such thick masses, must have been profoundly deep; but again the subterranean forces exerted themselves, and I now beheld the bed of that ocean forming a chain of mountains more than 7000 feet in height.

Vast, and scarcely comprehensible as such changes must ever appear, yet they have all occurred within a period, recent when compared with the history of the Cordillera; and the Cordillera itself is absolutely modern as compared with many of the fossiliferous strata of Europe and America. . . .

6 APRIL
In the morning we found some thief had stolen one of our mules, and the bell of the madrina. We therefore rode only two or three miles down the valley, and stayed there the ensuing day in hopes of recovering the mule, which the arriero thought had been hidden in some ravine. . . . On the 10th we reached Santiago, where I received a very kind and hospitable reception from Mr Caldcleugh. My excursion only cost me twenty-four days, and never did I more deeply enjoy an equal space of time.

[*From April to July 1835, while the* Beagle *continued her survey of the coast, Darwin made another land journey to Coquimbo and Copiapo, visiting silver and copper mines on the way. During July and August the* Beagle *concluded the survey work of the Peruvian coast, and finally set sail on 7 September for the Galapagos Islands.*]

The Galapagos Archipelago

JOURNAL 15 SEPTEMBER

This archipelago consists of ten principal islands, of which five exceed the others in size. They are situated under the Equator, and between five and six hundred miles westward of the coast of America. They are all formed of volcanic rocks: a few fragments of granite curiously glazed and altered by the heat can hardly be considered as an exception. Some of the craters surmounting the larger islands are of immense size, and they rise to a height of between three and four thousand feet. Their flanks are studded by innumerable smaller orifices. I scarcely hesitate to affirm, that there must be in the whole archipelago at least 2000 craters. These consist either of lava and scoriæ, or of finely-stratified, sandstone-like tuff [tufa]. Most of the latter are beautifully symmetrical; they owe their origin to eruptions of volcanic mud without any lava. It is a remarkable circumstance that every one of the twenty-eight tuff-craters which were examined had their southern sides either much lower than the other sides, or quite broken down and removed. As all these craters have apparently been formed when standing in the sea, and as the waves from the trade-wind and the swell from the open Pacific here unite their forces on the southern coasts of all the islands, this singular uniformity in the broken state of the craters, composed of the soft and yielding tuff, is easily explained.

Considering that these islands are placed directly under the equator, the climate is far from being excessively hot. This seems chiefly caused by the singularly low temperature of the surrounding water, brought here by the great southern Polar current. Excepting during one short season, very little rain falls, and even then it is irregular; but the clouds generally hang low. Hence, whilst the lower parts of the island are very sterile, the upper parts, at a height of 1000 feet and upwards, possess a damp climate and a tolerably luxuriant vegetation. This is especially the case on the windward sides of the islands, which first receive and condense the moisture from the atmosphere.

In the morning we landed on Chatham Island, which, like the others, rises with a tame and rounded outline, broken here and there by scattered hillocks, the remains of former craters. Nothing could be less inviting than the first appearance. A broken field of black basaltic lava, thrown into the most rugged waves and crossed by great fissures, is everywhere covered by stunted, sunburnt brushwood, which shows little signs of life. The dry and parched surface, being heated by the noonday sun, gave to the air a close and sultry feeling, like that from a stove. We fancied even that the bushes smelt unpleasantly. Although I diligently tried to collect as many plants as possible, I succeeded in getting very few, and such wretched-looking little weeds would have better become an arctic than an equatorial flora. . . .

The *Beagle* sailed round Chatham Island, and anchored in several bays. One night I slept on shore on a part of the island where black, truncated cones were extraordinarily numerous: from one small eminence I counted sixty of them, all surmounted by craters more or less perfect. The greater number consisted merely of a ring of red scoriæ or slags, cemented together, and their height above the plain of lava was not more than from fifty to a hundred feet. None had been very lately active. The entire surface of this part of the island seems to have been permeated, like a sieve, by the subterranean vapours: here and there the lava, whilst soft, has been blown into great bubbles, and in other parts the tops of caverns similarly formed have fallen in, leaving circular pits with steep sides. From the regular form of the many craters, they gave to the country an artificial appearance, which vividly reminded me of those parts of Staffordshire where the great iron-foundries are most numerous. The day was glowing-hot, and the scrambling over the rough surface and through the intricate thickets was very fatiguing; but I was well repaid by the strange Cyclopean scene. As I was walking along I met two large tortoises, each of which must have weighed at least two hundred pounds. One was eating a piece of cactus, and as I approached, it stared at me and slowly stalked away; the other gave a deep hiss, and drew in its head. These huge reptiles, surrounded by the black lava, the leafless shrubs, and large cacti, seemed to my fancy like some antediluvian animals. The few dull-coloured birds cared no more for me, than they did for the great tortoises.

23 SEPTEMBER

The *Beagle* proceeded to Charles Island. This archipelago has long been frequented, first by the buccaneers, and latterly by whalers, but it is only within the last six years that a small colony has been established here. The inhabitants are between two and three hundred in number: they are nearly all people of colour, who have been banished for political crimes from the Republic of the Equator, of which Quito is the capital. The settlement is placed about four and a half miles inland, and at a height probably of a thousand feet....

The inhabitants, although complaining of poverty, obtain without much trouble the means of subsistence. In the woods there are many wild pigs and goats, but the staple article of animal food is supplied by the tortoises. Their numbers have of course been greatly reduced in this island, but the people yet count on two days' hunting giving them food for the rest of the week. It is said that formerly single vessels have taken away as many as seven hundred, and that the ship's company of a frigate some years since brought down in one day 200 tortoises to the beach.

29 SEPTEMBER

We doubled the south-west extremity of Albemarle Island, and the next day were nearly becalmed between it and Narborough Island. Both are covered with immense deluges of black, naked lava, which have flowed either over the rims of the great caldrons, like pitch over the rim of a pot in which it has been boiled, or have burst forth from smaller orifices on the flanks. In their descent they have spread over miles of the sea-coast. On both of these islands, eruptions are known to have taken place; and in Albemarle, we saw a small jet of smoke curling from the summit of one of the great craters....

The rocks on the coast abounded with great black lizards, between three and four feet long; and on the hills, an ugly yellowish-brown species was equally common. We saw many of this latter kind, some clumsily running out of our way, and others shuffling into their burrows....

The natural history of these islands is eminently curious, and well deserves attention. Most of the organic productions are aboriginal creations, found nowhere else: there is even a difference between the inhabitants of the different islands. Yet all show a marked relationship with those of America, though separated from that continent by an open space of ocean, between 500 and 600 miles in width. The archipelago is a little world within itself, or rather a satellite attached to America, whence it has derived a few stray colonists, and has received the general character of its indigenous productions. Considering the small size of these islands, we feel the more astonished at the number of their aboriginal beings, and at their confined range. Seeing every height crowned with its crater, and the boundaries of most of the lava-streams still distinct, we are led to believe that within a period, geologically recent, the unbroken ocean was here spread out. Hence, both in space and time, we seem to be brought somewhat near to that great fact – that mystery of mysteries – the first appearance of new beings on this earth. . . .

Of land-birds I obtained twenty-six kinds, all peculiar to the group and found nowhere else, with the exception of one lark-like finch from North America (Dolichonyx oryzivorus), which ranges on that continent as far north as 54°, and generally frequents marshes. The other twenty-five birds consist, firstly, of a hawk, curiously intermediate in structure between a buzzard and the American group of carrion-feeding polybori; and with these latter birds it agrees most closely in every habit and even tone of voice. Secondly, there are two owls, representing the short-eared and white barn-owls of Europe. Thirdly, a wren, three tyrant fly-catchers (two of them species of pyrocephalus, one or both of which would be ranked by some ornithologists as only varieties), and a dove – all analogous to, but distinct from, American species. Fourthly, a swallow, which though differing from the Progne purpurea of both Americas only in being rather duller coloured, smaller and slenderer, is considered by Mr [John] Gould as specifically distinct. Fifthly, there are three species of mocking-thrush – a form highly characteristic of America.

The remaining land-birds form a most singular group of finches, related to each other in the structure of their beaks, short tails, form of body, and plumage: there are thirteen species, which Mr Gould has divided into four sub-groups. All these species are peculiar to this archipelago; and so is the whole group, with the exception of one species of the sub-group cactornis, lately brought from Bow Island, in the Low Archipelago. Of cactornis, the two species may be often seen climbing about the flowers of the great cactus-trees; but all the other species of this group of finches, mingled together in flocks, feed on the dry and sterile ground of the lower districts. The males of all, or certainly of the greater number, are jet black, and the females (with perhaps one or two exceptions) are brown. The most curious fact is the perfect gradation in the size of the beaks in the different species of geospiza, from one as large as that of a hawfinch to that of a chaffinch, and (if Mr Gould is right in including his sub-group, certhidea), even to that of a warbler. . . .

Of waders and water-birds I was able to get only eleven kinds, and of these only three (including a rail confined to the damp summits of the islands) are new species. Considering the wandering habits of the gulls, I was surprised to find that the species inhabiting these islands is peculiar,.but allied to one from the southern parts of South America. The far greater peculiarity of the land-birds, namely, twenty-five out of twenty-six being new species or at least new races, compared with the waders and web-footed birds, is in accordance with the greater range which these latter orders have in all parts of the world. . . .

We will now turn to the order of reptiles, which gives the most striking character to the zoology of these islands. The species are not numerous, but the numbers of individuals of each species are extra-ordinarily great. . . .

I will first describe the habits of the tortoise (Testudo nigra, for-merly called indica), which has been so frequently alluded to. These animals are found, I believe, on all the islands of the archipelago; certainly on the greater number. They frequent in preference the high, damp parts, but they likewise live in the lower and arid dis-tricts. I have already shown, from the numbers which have been caught in a single day, how very numerous they must be. Some grow to an immense size: Mr Lawson, an Englishman, and vice-governor of the colony, told us that he had seen several so large that it required six or eight men to lift them from the ground, and that some had afforded as much as 200 pounds of meat. The old males are the largest, the females rarely growing to so great a size: the male can readily be distinguished from the female by the greater length of its tail. The tortoises which live on those islands where there is no water, or in the lower and arid parts of the others, feed chiefly on the succu-lent cactus. Those which frequent the higher and damp regions, eat the leaves of various trees, a kind of berry (called guayavita) which is acid and austere, and likewise a pale green filamentous lichen (Usnera plicata), that hangs in tresses from the boughs of the trees.

The tortoise is very fond of water, drinking large quantities, and wallowing in the mud. The larger islands alone possess springs, and these are always situated towards the central parts, and at a consider-able height. The tortoises therefore which frequent the lower dis-tricts, when thirsty, are obliged to travel from a long distance. Hence broad and well-beaten paths branch off in every direction from the wells down to the sea-coasts and the Spaniards by following them up first discovered the watering-places.

When I landed at Chatham Island, I could not imagine what animal travelled so methodically along well-chosen tracks. Near the springs it was a curious spectacle to behold many of these huge creatures, one set eagerly travelling onwards with outstretched necks, and another set returning, after having drunk their fill. When the tortoise arrives at the spring, quite regardless of any spectator, he buries his head in the water above his eyes, and greedily swallows great mouthfuls, at the rate of about ten in a minute. The inhabitants say each animal stays three or four days in the neighbourhood of the water, and then returns to the lower country; but they differed respecting the frequency of these visits. The animal probably regulates them according to the nature of the food on which it has lived. It is, however, certain, that tortoises can subsist even on those islands where there is no other water than what falls during a few rainy days in the year.

I believe it is well ascertained that the bladder of the frog acts as a reservoir for the moisture necessary to its existence. Such seems to be the case with the tortoise. For some time after a visit to the springs, their urinary bladders are distended with fluid, which is said gradually to decrease in volume, and to become less pure. The inhabitants, when walking in the lower district, and overcome with thirst, often take advantage of this circumstance, and drink the contents of the bladder if full: in one I saw killed, the fluid was quite limpid, and had only a very slightly bitter taste. The inhabitants, however, always first drink the water in the pericardium, which is described as being best....

The inhabitants believe that these animals are absolutely deaf; certainly they do not overhear a person walking close behind them. I was always amused when overtaking one of these great monsters, as it was quietly pacing along, to see how suddenly, the instant I passed it, it would draw in its head and legs, and uttering a deep hiss fall to the ground with a heavy sound, as if struck dead. I frequently got on their backs, and then, giving a few raps on the hinder part of their shells, they would rise up and walk away – but I found it very difficult to keep my balance. The flesh of this animal is largely employed, both fresh and salted, and a beautifully clear oil is prepared from the fat. When a tortoise is caught, the man makes a slit in the skin near its tail, so as to see inside its body, whether the fat under the dorsal plate is thick. If it is not, the animal is liberated; and it is said to recover soon from this strange operation. In order to secure the tortoises, it is not sufficient to turn them like turtle, for they are often able to get on their legs again.

There can be little doubt that this tortoise is an aboriginal inhabitant of the Galapagos; for it is found on all, or nearly all, the islands, even on some of the smaller ones where there is no water. Had it been an imported species, this would hardly have been the case in a group which has been so little frequented. Moreover, the old buccaneers found this tortoise in greater numbers even than at present.... It is now widely distributed, but it may be questioned whether it is in any other place an aboriginal....

The amblyrhynchus, a remarkable genus of lizards, is confined to this archipelago: there are two species, resembling each other in general form, one being terrestrial and the other aquatic. This latter species (A. cristatus) was first characterised by Mr Bell, who well foresaw, from its short, broad head, and strong claws of equal length, that its habits of life would turn out very peculiar, and different from those of its nearest ally, the Iguana. It is extremely common on all the islands throughout the group, and lives exclusively on the rocky sea-beaches, being never found – at least I never saw one – even ten yards inshore. It is a hideous-looking creature, of a dirty black colour, stupid and sluggish in its movements. The usual length of a full-grown one is about a yard, but there are some even four feet long; a large one weighed twenty pounds. On the island of Albemarle they seem to grow to a greater size than elsewhere. Their tails are flattened sideways, and all four feet partially-webbed. They are occasionally seen some hundred yards from the shore, swimming about....

The nature of this lizard's food, as well as the structure of its tail and feet, and the fact of its having been seen voluntarily swimming out at sea, absolutely prove its aquatic habits; yet there is in this respect one strange anomaly, namely, that when frightened it will not enter the water.... I threw one several times as far as I could into a deep pool left by the retiring tide; but it invariably returned in a direct line to the spot where I stood. It swam near the bottom, with a very graceful and rapid movement, and occasionally aided itself over the uneven ground with its feet. As soon as it arrived near the edge, but still being under water, it tried to conceal itself in the tufts of seaweed, or it entered some crevice. As soon as it thought the danger was past, it crawled out on the dry rocks, and shuffled away as quickly as it could....

Perhaps this singular piece of apparent stupidity may be accounted for by the circumstance that this reptile has no enemy whatever on shore, whereas at sea it must often fall a prey to the numerous sharks. Hence, probably, urged by a fixed and hereditary instinct that the shore is its place of safety, whatever the emergency may be, it there takes refuge. . . .

We will now turn to the terrestrial species (A. demarlii), with a round tail, and toes without webs. This lizard, instead of being found like the other on all the islands, is confined to the central part of the archipelago, namely to Albemarle, James, Barrington and Indefatigable islands. . . . It would appear as if it had been created in the centre of the archipelago, and thence had been dispersed only to a certain distance. Some of these lizards inhabit the high and damp parts of the islands, but they are much more numerous in the lower and sterile districts near the coast. I cannot give a more forcible proof of their numbers than by stating that, when we were left at James Island, we could not for some time find a spot free from their burrows on which to pitch our single tent. Like their brothers the sea-kind, they are ugly animals, of a yellowish orange beneath and of a brownish red colour above: from their low facial angle they have a singularly stupid appearance. They are, perhaps, of a rather less size than the marine species, but several of them weighed between ten and fifteen pounds. In their movements they are lazy and half torpid. When not frightened, they slowly crawl along with their tails and bellies dragging on the ground. They often stop, and doze for a minute or two, with closed eyes and hind legs spread out on the parched soil. . . .

The botany of this group is fully as interesting as the zoology. . . . Of flowering plants there are, as far as at present is known, 185 species, and 40 cryptogamic species, making together 225; of this number I was fortunate enough to bring home 193. Of the flowering plants, 100 are new species, and are probably confined to this archipelago. . . . Of the plants not so confined, at least 10 species found near the cultivated ground at Charles Island, have been imported. It is, I think, surprising that more American species have not been introduced naturally, considering that the distance is only between 500 and 600 miles from the continent; and that drift-wood, bamboos, canes and the nuts of a palm, are often washed on the south-eastern shores. . . .

I have not as yet noticed by far the most remarkable feature in the natural history of this archipelago. It is, that the different islands to a considerable extent are inhabited by a different set of beings. My attention was first called to this fact by the vice-governor, Mr Lawson, declaring that the tortoises differed from the different islands, and that he could with certainty tell from which island any one was brought. I did not for some time pay sufficient attention to this statement, and I had already partially mingled together the collections from two of the islands. I never dreamed that islands, about fifty or sixty miles apart, and most of them in sight of each other, formed of precisely the same rocks, placed under a quite similar climate, rising to a nearly equal height, would have been differently tenanted; but...this is the case. It is the fate of most voyagers, no sooner to discover what is most interesting in any locality, than they are hurried from it; but I ought, perhaps, to be thankful that I obtained sufficient material to establish this most remarkable fact in the distribution of organic beings.

The inhabitants, as I have said, state that they can distinguish the tortoises from the different islands; and that they differ not only in size, but in other characters. Captain Porter has described those from Charles and from the nearest island to it, named Hood Island, as having their shells in front thick and turned up like a Spanish saddle, whilst the tortoises from James Island are rounder, blacker, and have a better taste when cooked.... My attention was first thoroughly aroused, by comparing together the numerous specimens, shot by myself and several other parties on board, of the mocking-thrushes, when, to my astonishment, I discovered that all those from Charles Island belonged to one species (Mimus trifasciatus); all from Albemarle Island to M. parvulus; and all from James and Chatham Islands (between which two other islands are situated, as connecting links) belonged to M. melanotis. These two latter species are closely allied, and would by some ornithologists be considered as only well-marked races or varieties; but the Mimus trifasciatus is very distinct. Unfortunately most of the specimens of the finch tribe were mingled together; but I have strong reasons to suspect that some of the species of the sub-group geospiza are confined to separate islands. If the different islands have their representatives of geospiza, it may help to explain the singularly large number of the species of this sub-group in this one small archipelago, and as a probable consequence of their numbers, the perfectly graduated series in the size of their beaks....

The distribution of the tenants of this archipelago would not be nearly so wonderful, if, for instance, one island had a mocking-thrush, and a second island some other quite distinct genus; if one island had its genus of lizard, and a second island another distinct genus, or none whatever; or if the different islands were inhabited, not by representative species of the same genera of plants, but by totally different genera, as does to a certain extent hold good: for, to give one instance, a large berry-bearing tree at James Island has no representative species in Charles Island. But it is the circumstance, that several of the islands possess their own species of the tortoise, mocking-thrush, finches, and numerous plants, these species having the same general habits, occupying analogous situations, and obviously filling the same place in the natural economy of this archipelago, that strikes me with wonder. It may be suspected that some of these representative species, at least in the case of the tortoise and of some of the birds, may hereafter prove to be only well-marked races; but this would be of equally great interest to the philosophical naturalist. . . .

The only light which I can throw on this remarkable difference in the inhabitants of the different islands, is, that very strong currents of the sea running in a westerly and west-north-west direction must separate, as far as transportal by the sea is concerned, the southern islands from the northern ones; and between these northern islands a strong north-west current was observed, which must effectually separate James and Albemarle Islands. As the archipelago is free to a most remarkable degree from gales of wind, neither the birds, insects, nor lighter seeds, would be blown from island to island. And lastly, the profound depth of the ocean between the islands, and their apparently recent (in a geological sense) volcanic origin, render it highly unlikely that they were ever united; and this, probably, is a far more important consideration than any other, with respect to the geographical distribution of their inhabitants.

Reviewing the facts here given, one is astonished at the amount of creative force, if such an expression may be used, displayed on these small, barren and rocky islands; and still more so at its diverse yet analogous action on points so near each other. I have said that the Galapagos Archipelago might be called a satellite attached to America, but it should rather be called a group of satellites, physically similar, organically distinct, yet intimately related to each other, and all related in a marked, though much lesser, degree to the great American continent.

[*On 20 October 1835 the* Beagle *left the Galapagos Islands, to begin the long journey home. She travelled by way of Tahiti, New Zealand, Australia, Mauritius, Cape of Good Hope, St Helena and Ascención Island, and made a brief return visit to Bahia, before landfall in Falmouth on 2 October 1836. Here Darwin left the 'good little vessel' on which he had lived for nearly five years.*

It was all interesting, but his Diary descriptions of this part of the voyage betray a certain weariness. In fact, although Darwin did not know it he had already made most of those observations which were to prove important. At the end of the Diary he wrote a kind of epilogue, summing up his main impressions of the voyage. As the Autobiography was to reveal (see page 161), ideas of the origin of species were already forming in his mind, but these serenely enthusiastic pages hint at nothing which would disturb even the most conventional Victorian reader.]

Nothing could be less inviting than the first appearance [of the Galapagos Archipelago]. *A broken field of black basaltic lava, thrown into the most rugged waves and crossed by great fissures.* ...

(p. 135)

The rocks on the coast abounded with great black lizards, between three and four feet long.
(p. 136)

The terrestrial species (A. Demarlii), with a round tail, and toes without webs ... like their brothers the sea-kind are ugly animals, of a yellowish orange beneath and of a brownish red colour above: from their low facial angle they have a singularly stupid appearance. (p. 141)

... *The perfect gradation in the size of the beaks in the different species of Geospiza, from one as large as that of a hawfinch to that of a chaffinch.* (p. 137)

The tortoises ... live chiefly on the succulent cactus. (p. 138)
When the tortoise arrives at the spring (below) *... he buries his head in the water above his eyes, and greeedily swallows great mouthfuls.* (p. 139)

HOOD ISLAND TORTOISE

GEOCHELONE ELEPHANTOPUS VANDENBURGHI

OPUNTIA

MICONIA ROBINSONIA

SESUVIUM EDMONSTONEI

PASSIFLORA FOETIDA

LICHENS

OPUNTIA ECHIOS

CHUCOCCA ALBA

Considering the wandering habits of the gulls, I was surprised to find that the species inhabiting these islands is peculiar [to it] ...
(p. 138)

The Traveller Returned

DIARY Our voyage having come to an end, I will take a short retrospect of the advantages and disadvantages, the pains and pleasures, of our five years' wandering.

If a person should ask my advice before undertaking a long voyage, my answer would depend upon his possessing a decided taste for some branch of knowledge which could by such means be acquired. No doubt it is a high satisfaction to behold various countries and the many races of mankind, but the pleasures gained at the time do not counterbalance the evils. It is necessary to look forward to a harvest however distant it may be, when some fruit will be reaped, some good effected. Many of the losses which must be experienced are obvious – such as that of the society of all old friends, and of the sight of those places, with which every dearest remembrance is so intimately connected. These losses, however, are at the time partly relieved by the exhaustless delight of anticipating the long-wished for day of return. If, as poets say, life is a dream, I am sure in a long voyage these are the visions which best pass away the long night. Other losses, although not at first felt, after a period tell heavily. These are the want of room, of seclusion, of rest, the jading feeling of constant hurry, the privation of small luxuries, the comforts of civilisation, domestic society, and lastly even of music and the other pleasures of imagination.

When such trifles are mentioned, it is evident that the real grievances (excepting from accidents) of a sea life are at an end. The short space of sixty years has made a most astonishing difference in the facility of distant navigation. Even in the time of Cook, a man who left his comfortable fireside for such expeditions, did undergo privations: a yacht with every luxury of life might now circumnavigate the globe. Besides the vast improvements in ships and naval resources, the whole Western shores of America are thrown open; and Australia is become a metropolis of a rising continent. How different are the circumstances to a man shipwrecked at the present day in the Pacific, to what they would have been in the time of Cook.

Since his voyage a hemisphere has been added to the civilised world.

If a person suffers much from sea sickness, let him weigh it heavily in the balance. I speak from experience; it is no trifling evil cured in a week, as most people suppose. If he takes pleasure in naval tactics, it will afford him full scope for his taste; but even the greater number of sailors, as it appears to me, have little real liking for the sea itself. It must be borne in mind how large a proportion of the time during a long voyage is spent on the water, as compared to the days in harbour. And what are the boasted glories of the illimitable ocean? A tedious waste, a desert of water, as the Arabian calls it. No doubt there are some delightful scenes; a moonlit night, with the clear heavens, the dark glittering sea, the white sails filled by the soft air of a gently blowing trade wind; a dead calm, the heaving surface polished like a mirror, and all quite still excepting the occasional flapping of the sails. It is well once to behold a squall, with its rising arch, and coming fury, or the heavy gale and mountainous waves. I confess, however, my imagination had painted something more grand, more terrific in the full grown storm. It is a finer sight on the canvas of Vandervelde, and infinitely finer when beheld on shore, where the waving trees, the wild flight of the birds, the dark shadows and bright lights, the rushing torrents, all proclaim the strife of the unloosed elements. At sea, the albatross and petrel fly as if the storm was their proper sphere, the water rises and sinks as if performing its usual task, the ship alone and its inhabitants seem the object of wrath. On a forlorn and weather-beaten coast, the scene is indeed different; but the feelings partake more of horror than of wild delight.

Let us now look at the brighter side of the past time. The pleasure derived from beholding the scenery and general aspect of the various countries we have visited, has decidedly been the most constant and highest source of enjoyment. It is probable that the picturesque beauty of many parts of Europe far exceeds anything we have beheld. But there is a growing pleasure in comparing the character of scenery in different countries, which to a certain degree is distinct from merely admiring their beauty. It more depends on an acquaintance with the individual parts of each view: I am strongly induced to believe that, as in music the person who understands every note, will, if he also has true taste, more thoroughly enjoy the whole, so he who examines each part of a fine view, may also thoroughly comprehend the full and combined effect. Hence a traveller should be a botanist, for in all views plants form the chief embellishment. Group masses of naked rocks, even in the wildest forms – for a time they may afford a sublime spectacle, but they will soon grow monotonous; paint them with bright and varied colours – they will become fantastic; clothe them with vegetation – they must form at least a decent, if not a most beautiful picture.

When I said that the scenery of Europe was probably superior to anything which we have beheld, I must except, as a class by itself, that of the intertropical regions. The two cannot be compared together; but I have already too often enlarged on the grandeur of these latter climates. As the force of impression frequently depends upon preconceived ideas, I may add that all mine were taken from the vivid descriptions in the *Personal Narrative* [of Alexander von Humboldt] which far exceed in merit anything I have ever read on the subject. Yet with these high-wrought ideas, my feelings were very remote from partaking of a tinge of disappointment on first landing on the coast of Brazil.

Amongst the scenes which are deeply impressed on my mind, none exceed in sublimity the primeval forests, undefaced by the hand of man, whether those of Brazil, where the powers of life are predominant, or those of Tierra del Fuego, where death and decay prevail. Both are temples filled with the varied productions of the God of Nature. No one can stand unmoved in these solitudes, without feeling that there is more in man than the mere breath of his body. In calling up images of the past, I find the plains of Patagonia most frequently cross before my eyes. Yet these plains are pronounced by all most wretched and useless. They are only characterised by negative possessions: without habitations, without water, without trees, without mountains, they support merely a few dwarf plants. Why then, and the case is not peculiar to myself, do these arid wastes take so firm possession of the memory? Why have not the still more level, green and fertile pampas, which are serviceable to mankind, produced an equal impression? I can scarcely analyse these feelings, but it must be partly owing to the free scope given to the imagination. They are boundless, for they are scarcely practicable, and hence unknown: they bear the stamp of having thus lasted for ages, and there appears no limit to their duration through future time. If, as the ancients supposed, the flat earth was surrounded by an impassable breadth of water, or by deserts heated to an intolerable excess, who would not look at these last boundaries to man's knowledge with deep, but ill defined sensations?

Lastly, of natural scenery, the views from lofty mountains, though certainly in one sense not beautiful, are very memorable. I remember looking down from the crest of the highest Cordillera. The mind, undisturbed by minute details, was filled by the stupendous dimensions of the surrounding masses.

Of individual objects, perhaps no one is more sure to create astonishment than the first sight in his native haunt of a real barbarian – of man in his lowest and most savage state. One's mind hurries back over past centuries, and then asks, could our progenitors be such as these? Men – whose very signs and expressions are less intelligible to us than those of the domesticated animals; who do not possess the instinct of those animals, nor yet appear to boast of human reason, or at least of arts consequent on that reason. I do not believe it is possible to describe or paint the difference of savage and civilised man. It is the difference between a wild and tame animal: and part of the interest in beholding a savage is the same which would lead every one to desire to see the lion in his desert, the tiger tearing his prey in the jungle, the rhinoceros on the wide plain, or the hippopotamus wallowing in the mud of some African river.

Amongst the other most remarkable spectacles which we have beheld, may be ranked the stars of the Southern hemisphere; the water-spout; the glacier leading its blue stream of ice in a bold precipice overhanging the sea; a lagoon island, raised by the coral-forming animalcule; an active volcano; the overwhelming effects of a violent earthquake. These latter phenomena perhaps possess for me a higher interest, from their intimate connection with the geological structure of the world. The earthquake must, however, be to everyone a most impressive event. The solid earth, considered from our earliest childhood as the very type of solidity, has oscillated like a thin crust beneath our feet and in seeing the most beautiful and laboured works of man in a moment overthrown, we feel the insignificance of his boasted power.

It has been said that the love of the chase is an inherent delight in man – a relic of an instinctive passion. If so, I am sure the pleasure of living in the open air, with the sky for a roof and the ground for a table, is part of the same feeling. It is the savage returning to his wild and native habits. I always look back to our boat cruises and my land journeys, when through unfrequented countries, with a kind of extreme delight, which no scenes of civilisation could create. I do not doubt every traveller must remember the glowing sense of happiness from the simple consciousness of breathing in a foreign clime where the civilised man has seldom or never trod.

There are several other sources of enjoyment in a long voyage, which are perhaps of a more reasonable nature. The map of the world ceases to be a blank; it becomes a picture full of the most varied and animated figures. Each part assumes its true dimensions: large continents are not looked at in the light of islands, or islands considered as mere specks, which in truth are larger than many kingdoms of Europe. Africa, or North and South America, are well-sounding names and easily pronounced, but it is not till having sailed for some weeks along small portions of their coasts, that one is thoroughly convinced, how large a piece of our immense world these names imply.

From seeing the present state, it is impossible not to look forward with high expectation to the future progress of nearly an entire hemisphere. The march of improvement, consequent on the introduction of Christianity, through the South Sea, probably stands by itself on the records of the world. It is the more striking when we remember that but sixty years since, Cook, whose most excellent judgment none will dispute, could foresee no prospect of such change. Yet these changes have now been effected by the philanthropic spirit of the English nation.

In the same quarter of the globe, Australia is rising, or indeed may be said to have risen, into a grand centre of civilisation which at some not very remote period, will rule the empress of the southern hemisphere. It is impossible for an Englishman to behold these distant colonies, without a high pride and satisfaction. To hoist the British flag seems to draw as a certain consequence, wealth, prosperity and civilisation.

In conclusion, it appears to me that nothing can be more improving to a young naturalist, than a journey in distant countries. It both sharpens and partly also allays that want and craving which, as Sir J. Herschel remarks, a man experiences although every corporeal sense is fully satisfied. The excitement from the novelty of objects, and the chance of success, stimulates him on to activity. Moreover, as a number of isolated facts soon become uninteresting, the habit of comparison leads to generalisation. On the other hand, as the traveller stays but a short space of time in each place, his description must generally consist of mere sketches, instead of detailed observation. Hence arises, as I have found to my cost, a constant tendency to fill up the wide gaps of knowledge by innacurate and superficial hypotheses.

But I have too deeply enjoyed the voyage not to recommend to any naturalist to take all chances, and to start on travels by land if possible, if otherwise, on a long voyage. He may feel assured he will meet with no difficulties or dangers (excepting in rare cases) nearly so bad as he beforehand imagined. In a moral point of view, the effect ought to be to teach him good-humoured patience, unselfishness, the habit of acting for himself, and of making the best of everything, or contentment: in short, he should partake of the characteristic qualities of the greater number of sailors. Travelling ought also to teach him to distrust others: but at the same time he will discover how many truly good-natured people there are, with whom he never before had, nor ever again will have, any further communication, yet who are ready to offer him the most disinterested assistance.

[*The account of the voyage in the Autobiography is more candid, especially with regard to the character of FitzRoy:*]

CHARACTER OF FITZROY FROM THE AUTOBIOGRAPHY

FitzRoy's temper was a most unfortunate one. This was shown not only by passion but by fits of long-continued moroseness against those who had offended him. His temper was usually worst in the early morning, and with his eagle eye he could generally detect something amiss about the ship, and was then unsparing in his blame. The junior officers when they relieved each other in the forenoon used to ask whether 'much hot coffee had been served out this morning' – which meant how was the Captain's temper? He was also somewhat suspicious and occasionally in very low spirits, on one occasion bordering on insanity. He seemed to me often to fail in sound judgment or common sense. He was extremely kind to me, but was a man very difficult to live with on the intimate terms which necessarily followed from our messing by ourselves in the same cabin. We had several quarrels, for when out of temper he was utterly unreasonable. For instance, early in the voyage at Bahia in Brazil he defended and praised slavery, which I abominated, and told me that he had just visited a great slave-owner, who had called up many of his slaves and asked them whether they were happy, and whether they wished to be free, and all answered 'No'. I then asked him, perhaps with a sneer, whether he thought that the answers of slaves in the presence of their master was worth anything. This made him excessively angry, and he said that, as I doubted his word, we could not live any longer together. I thought that I should have been compelled to leave the ship; but as soon as the news spread – which it did quickly, as the captain sent for the first lieutenant to assuage his anger by abusing me – I was deeply gratified by receiving an invitation from all the gunroom officers to mess with them. But after a few hours FitzRoy showed his usual magnanimity by sending an

Sketch of Fitzroy c. 1838 by Philip King the younger

officer to me with an apology and a request that I would continue to live with him.

I remember another instance of his candour. At Plymouth before we sailed he was extremely angry with a dealer in crockery who refused to exchange some article purchased in his shop: the Captain asked the man the price of a very expensive set of china and said, 'I should have purchased this if you had not been so disobliging.' As I knew that the cabin was amply stocked with crockery, I doubted whether he had any such intention, and I must have shown my doubts in my face, for I said not a word. After leaving the shop he looked at me saying, 'You do not believe what I have said,' and I was forced to own that it was so. He was silent for a few minutes and then said, 'You are right, and I acted wrongly in my anger at the blackguard.'

At Concepción in Chile, poor FitzRoy was sadly overworked and in very low spirits. He complained bitterly to me that he must give a great party to all the inhabitants of the place. I remonstrated and said that I could see no such necessity on his part under the circumstances. He then burst out into a fury, declaring that I was the sort of man who would receive any favours and make no return. I got up and left the cabin without saying a word, and returned to Concepción where I was then lodging. After a few days I came back to the ship and was received by the Captain as cordially as ever, for the storm had by that time quite blown over. The first lieutenant, however, said to me: 'Confound you, philosopher, I wish you would not quarrel with the skipper; the day you left the ship I was dead-tired (the ship was refitting) and he kept me walking the deck till midnight abusing you all the time.' The difficulty of living on good terms with a captain of a man-of-war is much increased by its being almost mutinous to answer him as one would answer anyone else; and by the awe in which he is held – or was held in my time, by all on board. . . .

I saw FitzRoy only occasionally after our return home, for I was always afraid of unintentionally offending him, and did so once, almost beyond mutual reconciliation. He was afterwards very indignant with me for having published so unorthodox a book (for he became very religious) as the *Origin of Species*. Towards the close of his life he was as I fear, much impoverished, and this was largely due to his generosity. Anyhow, after his death a subscription was raised to pay his debts. His end was a melancholy one, namely suicide, exactly like that of his uncle Lord Castlereagh, whom he resembled closely in manner and appearance.

His character was in several respects one of the most noble which I have ever known, though tarnished by grave blemishes.

These two years and three months were the most active ones which I ever spent, though I was occasionally unwell and so lost some time. After going backwards and forwards several times between Shrewsbury, Maer, Cambridge and London, I settled in lodgings at Cambridge on 13 December, where all my collections were under the care of Henslow. I stayed three months, and got my minerals and rocks examined by the aid of Prof. Miller.

I began preparing my Journal of travels, which was not hard work, as my manuscript Journal had been written with care, and my chief labour was making an abstract of my more interesting scientific results. I sent also, at the request of Lyell, a short account of my observations on the elevation of the coast of Chile to the Geological Society.

On 7 March 1837 I took lodgings in Great Marlborough Street in London and remained there for nearly two years until I was married. During these two years I finished my Journal, read several papers before the Geological Society, began preparing the manuscript for my *Geological Observations* and arranged for the publication of the *Zoology of the Voyage of the Beagle*. In July I opened my first note-book for facts in relation to *The Origin of Species*, about which I had long reflected, and never ceased working on for the next twenty years....

During these two years I was led to think much about religion. Whilst on board the *Beagle* I was quite orthodox, and I remember being heartily laughed at by several of the officers (though themselves orthodox) for quoting the Bible as an unanswerable authority on some point of morality. I suppose it was the novelty of the argument that amused them. But I had gradually come, by this time, to see that the Old Testament, from its manifestly false history of the world, with the Tower of Babel, the rainbow as a sign etc. etc., and from its attributing to God the feelings of a revengeful tyrant, was no more to be trusted than the sacred books of the Hindus, or the beliefs of any barbarian. The question then continually rose before my mind and would not be banished: is it credible that if God were now to make a revelation to the Hindus, would he permit it to be connected with the belief in Vishnu, Siva etc., as Christianity is connected with the Old Testament? This appeared to me utterly incredible.

By further reflecting that the clearest evidence would be requisite to make any sane man believe in the miracles by which Christianity is supported; that the more we know of the fixed laws of nature the more incredible do miracles become; that the men at that time were ignorant and credulous to a degree almost incomprehensible by us; that the Gospels cannot be proved to have been written simultaneously with the events; that they differ in many important details, far too important, as it seemed to me, to be admitted as the usual inaccuracies of eye-witnesses; by such reflections as these, which I give, not as having the least novelty or value, but as they influenced me, I gradually came to disbelieve in Christianity as a divine revelation. The fact that many false religions have spread over large portions of the earth like wild-fire had some weight with me. Beautiful as is the morality of the New Testament, it can hardly be denied that its perfection depends in part on the interpretation which we now put on metaphors and allegories.

But I was very unwilling to give up my belief: I feel sure of this, for I can well remember often and often inventing day-dreams of old letters between distinguished Romans and manuscripts being discovered at Pompeii or elsewhere which confirmed in the most striking manner all that was written in the Gospels. But I found it more and more difficult, with free scope given to my imagination, to invent evidence which would suffice to convince me. Thus disbelief crept over me at a very slow rate, but was at last complete. The rate was so slow that I felt no distress, and have never since doubted even for a single second that my conclusion was correct. I can indeed hardly see how anyone ought to wish Christiantity to be true; for if so the plain language of the text seems to show that the men who do not believe, and this would include my father, brother and almost all my best friends, will be everlastingly punished. And this is a damnable doctrine.

Although I did not think much about the existence of a personal God until a considerably later period of my life, I will here give the vague conclusions to which I have been driven. The old argument of design in nature, as given by Paley, which formerly seemed to me so conclusive, fails, now that the law of natural selection has been discovered. We can no longer argue that, for instance, the beautiful hinge of a bivalve shell must have been made by an intelligent being, like the hinge of a door by man. There seems to be no more design in the variability of organic beings and in the action of natural selection than in the course which the wind blows. Everything in nature is the result of fixed laws. . . .

But passing over the endless beautiful adaptations which we everywhere meet with, it may be asked how can the generally beneficent arrangement of the world be accounted for? Some writers indeed are so much impressed with the amount of suffering in the world, that they doubt if we look to all sentient beings, whether there is more of misery or of happiness; whether the world as a whole is a good or a bad one. According to my judgment, happiness decidedly prevails, though this would be very difficult to prove. If the truth of this conclusion be granted, it harmonises well with the effects which we might expect from natural selection. If all the individuals of any species were habitually to suffer to an extreme degree they would neglect to propagate their kind; but we have no reason to believe that this has ever or at least often occurred. Some other considerations, moreover, lead to the belief that all sentient beings have been formed so as to enjoy, as a general rule, happiness.

Every one who believes, as I do, that all the corporeal and mental organs (excepting those which are neither advantageous or disadvantageous to the possessor) of all beings have been developed through natural selection, or the survival of the fittest, together with use or habit, will admit that these organs have been formed so that their possessors may compete successfully with other beings, and thus increase in number. Now an animal may be led to pursue that course of action which is the most beneficial to the species by suffering – such as pain, hunger, thirst and fear – or by pleasure – as in eating and drinking and in the propagation of the species etc., or by both means combined, as in the search for food.

But pain or suffering of any kind, if long continued, causes depression and lessens the power of action; yet is well adapted to make a creature guard itself against any great or sudden evil. Pleasurable sensations, on the other hand, may be long continued without any depressing effect; on the contrary they stimulate the whole system to increased action. Hence it has come to pass that most or all sentient beings have been developed in such a manner, through natural selection, that pleasurable sensations serve as their habitual guides. We see this in the pleasure from exertion, even occasionally from great exertion of the body or mind – in the pleasure of our daily meals, and especially in the pleasure derived from sociability and from loving our families. The sum of such pleasures as these, which are habitual or frequently recurrent, give, as I can hardly doubt, to most sentient beings an excess of happiness over misery, although many occasionally suffer much. Such suffering, is quite compatible with the belief in natural selection, which is not perfect in its action, but tends only to render each species as successful as possible in the battle for life with other species, in wonderfully complex and changing circumstances.

That there is much suffering in the world no one disputes. Some have attempted to explain this in reference to man by imagining that it serves for his moral improvement. But the number of men in the world is as nothing compared with that of all other sentient beings, and these often suffer greatly without any moral improvement. A being so powerful and so full of knowledge as a God who could create the universe is to our finite minds omnipotent and omniscient, and it revolts our understanding to suppose that his benevolence is not unbounded, for what advantage can there be in the sufferings of millions of the lower animals throughout almost endless time? This very old argument from the existence of suffering against the existence of an intelligent first cause seems to me a strong one; whereas, as just remarked, the presence of much suffering agrees well with the view that all organic beings have been developed through variation and natural selection.

At the present day the most usual argument for the existence of an intelligent God is drawn from the deep inward conviction and feelings which are experienced by most persons. But it cannot be doubted that Hindus, Mohammedans and others might argue in the same manner and with equal force in favour of the existence of one god, or of many gods, or, as with the Buddhists, of no god. There are also many barbarian tribes who cannot be said with any truth to believe in what we call God: they believe indeed in spirits or ghosts, and it can be explained, as Tyler and Herbert Spencer have shown, how such a belief would be likely to arise.

Formerly I was led by feelings such as those just referred to (although I do not think that the religious sentiment was ever stronger developed in me), to the firm conviction of the existence of God, and of the immortality of the soul. In my Journal I wrote that whilst standing in the midst of the grandeur of a Brazilian forest, 'it is not possible to give an adequate idea of the higher feelings of wonder, admiration, and devotion which fill and elevate the mind'. I well remember my conviction that there is more in man than the mere breath of his body. But now the grandest scenes would not cause any such convictions and feelings to rise in my mind. It may be truly said that I am like a man who has become colour-blind, and the universal belief by men of the existence of redness makes my present loss of perception of not the least value as evidence. This argument would be a valid one if all men of all races had the same inward conviction of the existence of one God, but we know that this is very far from being the case. Therefore I cannot see that such inward convictions and feelings are of any weight as evidence of what really exists. The state of mind which grand scenes formerly excited in me, and which was intimately connected with a belief in God, did not essentially differ from that which is often called the sense of sublimity; and however difficult it may be to explain the genesis of this sense, it can hardly be advanced as an argument for the existence of God, any more than the powerful though vague and similar feelings excited by music. . . .

Another source of conviction in the existence of God, connected with the reason and not with the feelings, impresses me as having much more weight. This follows from the extreme difficulty or rather impossibility of conceiving this immense and wonderful universe, including man with his capacity of looking far backwards and far into futurity, as the result of blind chance or necessity. When thus reflecting, I feel compelled to look to a First Cause having an intelligent mind in some degree analogous to that of man; and I deserve to be called a Theist.

This conclusion was strong in my mind about the time, as far as I can remember, when I wrote *The Origin of Species*; and it is since that time that it has very gradually with many fluctuations become weaker. But then arises the doubt: can the mind of man, which has, as I fully believe, been developed from a mind as low as that possessed by the lowest animal, be trusted when it draws such grand conclusions? May not these be the result of the connection between cause and effect which strikes us as a necessary one, but probably depends merely on inherited experience? Nor must we overlook the probability of the constant inculcation in a belief in God on the minds of children producing so strong and perhaps an inherited effect on their brains not yet fully developed, that it would be as difficult for them to throw off their belief in God, as for a monkey to throw off its instinctive fear and hatred of a snake.

I cannot pretend to throw the least light on such abstruse problems. The mystery of the beginning of all things is insoluble by us; and I for one must be content to remain an agnostic.

[*In January 1839 Darwin married his cousin Emma Wedgwood, youngest daughter of his Uncle Jos. Their first home was in Upper Gower Street, London, where they lived until September 1842.*]

During the early part of our life in London, I was strong enough to go into general society, and saw a good deal of several scientific men and other more or less distinguished men. I will give my impressions with respect to some of them, though I have little worth saying. . . .

I saw more of [Sir Charles] Lyell [the geologist] than of any other man both before and after my marriage. His mind was characterised, as it appeared to me, by clearness, caution, sound judgment and a good deal of originality. When I made any remark to him on geology, he never rested until he saw the whole case clearly and often made me see it more clearly than I had done before. He would advance all possible objections to my suggestions, and even after these were exhausted would long remain dubious. A second characteristic was his hearty sympathy with the work of other scientific men. . . .

I often saw [Sir Richard] Owen [the palaeontologist], whilst living in London, and admired him greatly, but was never able to understand his character and never became intimate with him. After the publication of the *Origin of Species* he became my bitter enemy, not owing to any quarrel between us, but as far as I could judge out of jealousy at its success. Poor dear [Hugh] Falconer [a fellow scientist] had a very bad opinion of him, being convinced that he was not only ambitious, very envious and arrogant, but untruthful and dishonest. His power of hatred was certainly unsurpassed. When in former days I used to defend Owen, Falconer often said, 'You will find him out some day,' and so it has proved.

At a somewhat later period I became very intimate with [Dr Joseph] Hooker [the botanist], who has been one of my best friends throughout life. He is a delightfully pleasant companion and most kind-hearted. One can see at once that he is honourable to the backbone. His intellect is very acute, and he has great power of generalisation. He is the most untirable worker that I have ever seen, and will sit the whole day working with the microscope, and be in the evening as fresh and pleasant as ever. He is in all ways impulsive and somewhat peppery in temper, but the clouds pass away almost immediately. He once sent me an almost savage letter from a cause which will appear ludicrously small to an outsider, viz. because I maintained for a time the silly notion that our coal-plants had lived in shallow water in the sea. His indignation was all the greater because he could not pretend that he should ever have suspected that the mangrove (and a few other marine plants which I named) had lived in the sea, if they had been found only in a fossil state. On another occasion he was almost equally indignant because I rejected with scorn the notion that a continent had formerly extended between Australia and South America. I have known hardly any man more lovable than Hooker.

A little later I became intimate with Thomas Huxley. His mind is as quick as a flash of lightning and as sharp as a razor. He is the best talker whom I have known. He never writes and never says anything flat. From his conversation no one would suppose that he could cut up his opponents in so trenchant a manner as he can do and does do. He has been a most kind friend to me and would always take any trouble for me. He has been the mainstay in England of the principle of the gradual evolution of organic beings. Much splendid work as he has done in zoology, he would have done far more, if his time had not been so largely consumed by official and literary work, and by his efforts to improve the education of the country. He would allow me to say anything to him: many years ago I thought that it was a pity that he attacked so many scientific men, although I believe that he was right in each particular case, and I said so to him. He denied the charge indignantly, and I answered that I was very glad to hear that I was mistaken. . . .

DARWIN'S RETROSPECT OF HIS LIFE AFTER THE MOVE TO DOWN HOUSE, KENT, FROM THE AUTOBIOGRAPHY

After several fruitless searches in Surrey and elsewhere, we found this house [at Down] and purchased it. I was pleased with the diversified appearance of the vegetation proper to a chalk district, and so unlike what I had been accustomed to in the Midland counties; and still more pleased with the extreme quietness and rusticity of the place. It is not, however, quite so retired a place as a writer in a German periodical makes it, who says that my house can be approached only by a mule-track! Our fixing ourselves here has answered admirably in one way which we did not anticipate, namely by being very convenient for frequent visits from our children, who never miss an opportunity of doing so when they can.

Few persons can have lived a more retired life than we have done. Besides short visits to the houses of relations, and occasionally to the seaside or elsewhere, we have gone nowhere. During the first part of our residence we went a little into society, and received a few friends here; but my health almost always suffered from the excitement, violent shivering and vomiting attacks being thus brought on. I have therefore been compelled for many years to give up all dinner-parties; and this has been somewhat of a deprivation to me, as such parties always put me into high spirits. From the same cause I have been able to invite here very few scientific acquaintances. Whilst I was young and strong I was capable of very warm attachments, but of late years, though I still have very friendly feelings towards many persons, I have lost the power of becoming deeply attached to anyone, not even so deeply to my good and dear friends Hooker and Huxley, as I should formerly have been. As far as I can judge this grievous loss of feeling has gradually crept over me, from the expectation of much distress afterwards from exhaustion having become firmly associated in my mind with seeing and talking with anyone for an hour, except my wife and children.

My chief enjoyment and sole employment throughout life has been scientific work; and the excitement from such work makes me for the time forget, or drives quite away, my daily discomfort. I have therefore nothing to record during the rest of my life, except the publication of my several books. Perhaps a few details [of] how they arose may be worth giving.

In the early part of 1844 my observations on the volcanic islands visited during the voyage of the *Beagle* were published. In 1845, I took much pains in correcting a new edition of my *Journal of Researches*, which was originally published in 1839 as part of Fitz-Roy's work. The success of this my first literary child always tickles my vanity more than that of any of my other books. Even to this day it sells steadily in England and the United States, and has been translated for the second time into German, and into French and other languages. This success of a book of travels, especially of a scientific one, so many years after its first publication, is surprising. Ten thousand copies have now been sold in England of the second edition. In 1846 my *Geological Observations on South America* were published. I record in a little diary, which I have always kept, that my three geological books (*Coral Reefs* included) consumed four and a half years' steady work; 'and now it is ten years since my return to England. How much time have I lost by illness? . . .'

From September 1854 onwards I devoted all my time to arranging my huge pile of notes, to observing, and experimenting, in relation to the transmutation of species. During the voyage of the *Beagle* I had been deeply impressed by discovering in the pampean formation great fossil animals covered with armour like that on the existing armadillos; secondly, by the manner in which closely allied animals replace one another in proceeding southwards over the continent; and thirdly, by the South American character of most of the productions of the Galapagos archipelago, and more especially by the manner in which they differ slightly on each island of the group, none of these islands appearing to be very ancient in a geological sense.

It was evident that such facts as these, as well as many others, could be explained it seemed to me almost useless to endeavour to modified; and the subject haunted me. But it was equally evident that neither the action of the surrounding conditions nor the will of the organisms (especially in the case of plants) could account for the innumerable cases in which organisms of every kind are beautifully adapted to their habits of life – for instance, a woodpecker or tree-frog to climb trees, or a seed for dispersal by hooks or plumes. I had always been much struck by such adaptations, and until these could be explained it seemed to me almost useless to endeavour to prove by indirect evidence that species have been modified.

After my return to England it appeared to me that by following the example of Lyell in geology, and by collecting all facts which bore in any way on the variation of animals and plants under domestication and nature, some light might perhaps be thrown on the whole subject. My first note-book was opened in July 1837. I worked on true Baconian principles, and without any theory collected facts on a wholesale scale, more especially with respect to domesticated productions, by printed enquiries, by conversation with skilful breeders and gardeners, and by extensive reading. When I see the list of books of all kinds which I read and abstracted, including whole series of Journals and Transactions, I am surprised at my industry. I soon perceived that selection was the keystone of man's success in making useful races of animals and plants. But how selection could be applied to organisms living in a state of nature remained for some time a mystery to me.

In October 1838 – that is, fifteen months after I had begun my systematic enquiry – I happened to read for amusement Malthus on *Population*, and being well prepared to appreciate the struggle for existence which everywhere goes on from long-continued observation of the habits of animals and plants, it at once struck me that under these circumstances favourable variations would tend to be preserved, and unfavourable ones to be destroyed. The result of this would be the formation of new species. Here, then, I had at last got a theory by which to work; but I was so anxious to avoid prejudice, that I determined not for some time to write even the briefest sketch of it. In June 1842 I first allowed myself the satisfaction of writing a very brief abstract of my theory in pencil in thirty-five pages; and this was enlarged during the summer of 1844 into one of 230 pages, which I had fairly copied out and still possess.

But at that time I overlooked one problem of great importance;

and it is astonishing to me, except on the principle of Columbus and his egg, how I could have overlooked it and its solution. This problem is the tendency in organic beings descended from the same stock to diverge in character as they become modified. That they have diverged greatly is obvious from the manner in which species of all kinds can be classed under genera, genera under families, families under sub-orders, and so forth; and I can remember the very spot in the road, whilst in my carriage, when to my joy the solution occurred to me; and this was long after I had come to Down. The solution, as I believe, is that the modified offspring of all dominant and increasing forms tend to become adapted to many and highly diversified places in the economy of nature.

Early in 1856 Lyell advised me to write out my views pretty fully, and I began at once to do so on a scale three or four times as extensive as that which was afterwards followed in my *Origin of Species*; yet it was only an abstract of the materials which I had collected, and I got through about half the work on this scale. But my plans were overthrown, for early in the summer of 1858 Mr Wallace, who was then in the Malay archipelago, sent me an essay *On the Tendency of Varieties to depart indefinitely from the Original Type*; and this essay contained exactly the same theory as mine. Mr Wallace expressed the wish that if I thought well of his essay, I should send it to Lyell for perusal.

The circumstances under which I consented at the request of Lyell and Hooker to allow of an extract from my manuscript, together with a letter to Asa Gray, dated 5 September 1857, to be published at the same time with Wallace's Essay, are given in the *Journal of the Proceedings of the Linnean Society*, 1858, p. 45. I was at first very unwilling to consent, as I thought Mr Wallace might consider my doing so unjustifiable, for I did not then know how generous and noble was his disposition. The extract from my manuscript and the letter to Asa Gray had neither been intended for publication, and were badly written. Mr Wallace's essay, on the other hand, was admirably expressed and quite clear. Nevertheless, our joint productions excited very little attention, and the only published notice of them which I can remember was by Professor Haughton of Dublin, whose verdict was that all that was new in them was false, and what was true was old. This shows how necessary it is that any new view should be explained at considerable length in order to arouse public attention.

In September 1858 I set to work by the strong advice of Lyell and Hooker to prepare a volume on the transmutation of species, but was often interrupted by ill-health, and short visits to Dr Lane's delightful hydropathic establishment at Moor Park. I abstracted the manuscript begun on a much larger scale in 1856, and completed the volume on the same reduced scale. It cost me thirteen months' and ten days' hard labour. It was published under the title of *The Origin of Species* in November 1859. Though considerably added to and corrected in the later editions, it has remained substantially the same book.

It is no doubt the chief work of my life. It was from the first highly successful. The first small edition of 1250 copies was sold on the day of publication, and second edition of 3000 copies soon afterwards. Sixteen thousand copies have now (1876) been sold in England and considering how stiff a book it is, this is a large sale. It has been translated into almost every European tongue, even into such languages as Spanish, Bohemian, Polish, and Russian. . . . Even an essay in Hebrew has appeared on it, showing that the theory is contained in the Old Testament! The reviews were very numerous. For a time I collected all that appeared on the *Origin* and on my related books, and these amount (excluding newspaper reviews) to 265; but after a time I gave up the attempt in despair. Many separate essays and books on the subject have appeared; and in Germany a catalogue or bibliography on 'Darwinismus' has appeared every year or two.

The success of the *Origin* may, I think, be attributed in large part to my having long before written two condensed sketches, and to my having finally abstracted a much larger manuscript, which was itself an abstract. By this means I was enabled to select the more striking facts and conclusions. I had, also, during many years, followed a golden rule, namely, that whenever a published fact, a new observation or thought came across me, which was opposed to my general results, to make a memorandum of it without fail and at once; for I had found by experience that such facts and thoughts were far more apt to escape from the memory than favourable ones. Owing to this habit, very few objections were raised against my views which I had not at least noticed and attempted to answer.

It has sometimes been said that the success of the *Origin* proved 'that the subject was in the air,' or 'that men's minds were prepared for it'. I do not think that this is strictly true, for I occasionally sounded not a few naturalists, and never happened to come across a single one who seemed to doubt the permanence of species. Even Lyell and Hooker, though they would listen with interest to me, never seemed to agree. I tried once or twice to explain to able men what I meant by natural selection, but signally failed. What I believe was strictly true is that innumerable well-observed facts were stored in the minds of naturalists, ready to take their proper places as soon as any theory which would receive them was sufficiently explained. Another element in the success of the book was its moderate size; and this I owe to the appearance of Mr Wallace's essay; had I published on the scale in which I began to write in 1856, the book would have been four or five times as large as the *Origin*, and very few would have had the patience to read it.

I gained much by my delay in publishing from about 1839, when the theory was clearly conceived, to 1859; and I lost nothing by it, for I cared very little whether men attributed most originality to me or Wallace, and his essay no doubt aided in the reception of the theory. I was forestalled in only one important point, which my vanity has always made me regret, namely, the explanation by means of the Glacial period of the presence of the same species of plants and of some few animals on distant mountain summits and in the arctic regions. This view pleased me so much that I wrote it out *in extenso*, and it was read by Hooker some years before E. Forbes published his celebrated memoir on the subject. In the very few points in which we differed, I still think that I was in the right. I have never, of course, alluded in print to my having independently worked out this view.

Hardly any point gave me so much satisfaction when I was at work on the *Origin*, as the explanation of the wide difference in many classes between the embryo and the adult animal, and of the close resemblance of the embryos within the same class. No notice of this point was taken, as far as I remember, in the early reviews of the *Origin*, and I recollect expressing my surprise on this head in a letter to Asa Gray. Within late years several reviewers have given the whole credit of the idea to Fritz Müller and Häckel, who undoubtedly have worked it out much more fully, and in some respects more correctly than I did. I had materials for a whole chapter on the subject, and I ought to have made the discussion longer, for it is clear that I failed to impress my readers; and he who succeeds in doing so deserves, in my opinion, all the credit.

This leads me to remark that I have almost always been treated honestly by my reviewers, passing over those without scientific knowledge as not worthy of notice. My views have often been grossly misrepresented, bitterly opposed and ridiculed, but this has been generally done, as I believe, in good faith. . . . On the whole I do not doubt that my works have been over and over again greatly overpraised. I rejoice that I have avoided controversies, and this I owe to Lyell, who many years ago, in reference to my geological works, strongly advised me never to get entangled in a controversy, as it rarely did any good and caused a miserable loss of time and temper.

Whenever I have found out that I have blundered, or that my work has been imperfect, and when I have been contemptuously criticised, and even when I have been overpraised, so that I have felt mortified, it has been my greatest comfort to say hundreds of times to myself that 'I have worked as hard and as well as I could, and no man can do more than this.' I remember when in Good Success Bay, in Tierra del Fuego, thinking (and I believe that I wrote home to the effect) that I could not employ my life better than in adding a little to natural science. This I have done to the best of my abilities, and critics may say what they like, but they cannot destroy this conviction....

[During the year 1862] I published in the *Journal of the Linnean Society*, a paper *On the Two Forms, or Dimorphic Condition of Primula*, and during the next five years, five other papers on dimorphic and trimorphic plants. I do not think anything in my scientific life has given me so much satisfaction as making out the meaning of the structure of these plants. I had noticed in 1838 or 1839 the dimorphism of *Linum flavum*, and had at first thought that it was merely a case of unmeaning variability. But on examining the common species of primula, I found that the two forms were much too regular and constant to be thus viewed. I therefore became almost convinced that the common cowslip and primrose were on the high-road to become diœcious; – that the short pistil in the one form, and the short stamens in the other form were tending towards abortion. The plants were therefore subjected under this point of view to trial; but as soon as the flowers with short pistils fertilised with pollen from the short stamens, were found to yield more seeds than any other of the four possible unions, the abortion-theory was knocked on the head. After some additional experiment, it became evident that the two forms, though both were perfect hermaphrodites, bore almost the same relation to one another as do the two sexes of an ordinary animal....

My *Descent of Man* was published in February 1871. As soon as I had become, in the year 1837 or 1838, convinced that species were mutable productions, I could not avoid the belief that man must come under the same law. Accordingly I collected notes on the subject for my own satisfaction, and not for a long time with any intention of publishing. Although in *The Origin of Species* the derivation of any particular species is never discussed, yet I thought it best, in order that no honourable man should accuse me of concealing my views, to add that by the work in question 'light would be thrown on the origin of man and his history'. It would have been useless and injurious to the success of the book to have paraded without giving any evidence my conviction with respect to his origin.

But when I found that many naturalists fully accepted the doctrine of the evolution of species, it seemed to me advisable to work up such notes as I possessed and to publish a special treatise on the origin of man. I was the more glad to do so, as it gave me an opportunity of fully discussing sexual selection – a subject which had always greatly interested me. This subject, and that of the variation of our domestic productions, together with the causes and laws of variation, inheritance etc., and the intercrossing of plants, are the sole subjects which I have been able to write about in full, so as to use all the materials which I had collected. *The Descent of Man* took me three years to write, but then as usual some of this time was lost by ill-health, and some was consumed by preparing new editions and other minor works. A second and largely corrected edition of the *Descent* appeared in 1874.

My book on the *Expression of the Emotions in Men and Animals* was published in the autumn of 1872. I had intended to give only a chapter on the subject in the *Descent of Man*, but as soon as I began to put my notes together, I saw that it would require a separate treatise. My first child was born on 27 December 1839, and I at once commenced to make notes on the first dawn of the various expressions which he exhibited, for I felt convinced, even at this early period, that the most complex and fine shades of expression must all have had a gradual and natural origin. During the summer of the following year, 1840, I read Sir C. Bell's admirable work on Expression, and this greatly increased the interest which I felt in the subject, though I could not at all agree with his belief that various muscles had been specially created for the sake of expression. From this time forward I occasionally attended to the subject, both with respect to man and our domesticated animals. My book sold largely, 5267 copies having been disposed of on the day of publication.

In the summer of 1860 I was idling and resting near Hartfield, where two species of drosera abound; and I noticed that numerous insects had been entrapped by the leaves. I carried home some plants, and on giving them insects saw the movements of the tentacles, and this made me think it probable that the insects were caught for some special purpose. Fortunately a crucial test occurred to me, that of placing a large number of leaves in various nitrogenous and non-nitrogenous fluids of equal density; and as soon as I found that the former alone excited energetic movements, it was obvious that here was a fine new field for investigation.

During subsequent years, whenever I had leisure, I pursued my experiments, and my book on *Insectivorous Plants* was published in July 1875 – that is sixteen years after my first observations. The delay in this case, as with all my other books, has been a great advantage to me; for a man after a long interval can criticise his own work almost as well as if it were that of another person. The fact that a plant should secrete, when properly excited, a fluid containing an acid and ferment, closely analogous to the digestive fluid of an animal, was certainly a remarkable discovery....

Little remains to be said. I am not conscious of any change in my mind during the last thirty years, excepting in one point presently to be mentioned; nor indeed could any change have been expected unless one of general deterioration. But my father lived to his eighty-third year with his mind as lively as ever it was, and all his faculties undimmed, and I hope that I may die before my mind fails to a sensible extent. I think that I have become a little more skilful in guessing right explanations and in devising experimental tests; but this may probably be the result of mere practice, and of a larger store of knowledge. I have as much difficulty as ever in expressing myself clearly and concisely, and this difficulty has caused me a very great loss of time; but it has had the compensating advantage of forcing me to think long and intently about every sentence, and thus I have been often led to see errors in reasoning and in my own observations or those of others.

There seems to be a sort of fatality in my mind leading me to put at first my statement and proposition in a wrong or awkward form. Formerly I used to think about my sentences before writing them down, but for several years I have found that it saves time to scribble in a vile hand whole pages as quickly as I possibly can, contracting half the words, and then correct deliberately. Sentences thus scribbled down are often better ones than I could have written deliberately....

I have said that in one respect my mind has changed during the last twenty or thirty years. Up to the age of thirty, or beyond it, poetry of many kinds, such as the works of Milton, Gray, Byron, Wordsworth, Coleridge, and Shelley, gave me great pleasure, and even as a schoolboy I took intense delight in Shakespeare, especially in the historical plays. I have also said that formerly pictures gave me considerable, and music very great delight. But now for many years I cannot endure to read a line of poetry: I have tried lately to read Shakespeare, and found it so intolerably dull that it nauseated me. I have also almost lost any taste for pictures or music. Music generally sets me thinking too energetically on what I have been at work on; instead of giving me pleasure. I retain some taste for fine scenery, but it does not cause me the exquisite delight which it formerly did. On the other hand, novels which are works of the imagination, though not of a very high order, have been for years a wonderful relief and pleasure to me, and I often bless all novelists. A surprising number have been read aloud to me, and I like all if moderately good, and if they do not end unhappily – against which a law ought to be passed. A novel, according to my taste, does not come into the first class unless it contains some person whom one can thoroughly love, and if it be a pretty woman all the better.

This curious and lamentable loss of the higher aesthetic tastes is all the odder, as books on history, biographies and travels (independently of any scientific facts which they may contain), and essays on all sorts of subjects interest me as much as ever they did. My mind seems to have become a kind of machine for grinding general laws out of large collections of facts, but why this should have caused the atrophy of that part of the brain alone on which the higher tastes depend, I cannot conceive. A man with a mind more highly-organised or better-constituted than mine, would not I suppose have thus suffered; and if I had to live my life again I would have made a rule to read some poetry and listen to some music at least once every week; for perhaps the parts of my brain now atrophied could thus have been kept active through use. The loss of these tastes is a loss of happiness, and may possibly be injurious to the intellect, and more probably to the moral character, by enfeebling the emotional part of our nature.

My books have sold largely in England, have been translated into many languages, and passed through several editions in foreign countries. I have heard it said that the success of a work abroad is the best test of its enduring value. I doubt whether this is at all trustworthy; but judged by this standard my name ought to last for a few years. Therefore it may be worth while for me to try to analyse the mental qualities and the conditions on which my success has depended, though I am aware that no man can do this correctly.

I have no great quickness of apprehension or wit which is so remarkable in some clever men – for instance, Huxley. I am therefore a poor critic: a paper or book, when first read, generally excites my admiration, and it is only after considerable reflection that I perceive the weak points. My power to follow a long and purely abstract train of thought is very limited; I should, moreover, never have succeeded with metaphysics or mathematics. My memory is extensive, yet hazy: it suffices to make me cautious by vaguely telling me that I have observed or read something opposed to the conclusion which I am drawing, or on the other hand in favour of it; and after a time I can generally recollect where to search for my authority. So poor in one sense is my memory, that I have never been able to remember for more than a few days a single date or a line of poetry.

Some of my critics have said, 'Oh, he is a good observer, but has no power of reasoning.' I do not think that this can be true, for the *Origin of Species* is one long argument from the beginning to the end, and it has convinced not a few able men. No one could have written it without having some power of reasoning. I have a fair share of invention and of common sense or judgment, such as every fairly successful lawyer or doctor must have, but not I believe, in any higher degree.

On the favourable side of the balance, I think that I am superior to the common run of men in noticing things which easily escape attention, and in observing them carefully. My industry has been nearly as great at it could have been in the observation and collection of facts. What is far more important, my love of natural science has been steady and ardent. This pure love has, however, been much aided by the ambition to be esteemed by my fellow naturalists. From my early youth I have had the strongest desire to understand or explain whatever I observed – that is, to group all facts under some general laws. These causes combined have given me the patience to reflect or ponder for any number of years over any unexplained problem.

As far as I can judge, I am not apt to follow blindly the lead of other men. I have steadily endeavoured to keep my mind free, so as to give up any hypothesis, however much beloved (and I cannot resist forming one on every subject), as soon as facts are shown to be opposed to it. Indeed I have had no choice but to act in this manner, for with the exception of the Coral Reefs, I cannot remember a single first-formed hypothesis which had not after a time to be given up or greatly modified. This has naturally led me to distrust greatly deductive reasoning in the mixed sciences. On the other hand, I am not very sceptical, a frame of mind which I believe to be injurious to the progress of science. A good deal of scepticism in a scientific man is advisable to avoid much loss of time; for I have met with not a few men, who I feel sure have often thus been deterred from experiment or observations, which would have proved directly or indirectly serviceable. . . .

Lastly, I have had ample leisure from not having to earn my own bread. Even ill-health, though it has annihilated several years of my life, has saved me from the distractions of society and amusement.

Therefore, my success as a man of science, whatever this may have amounted to, has been determined, as far as I can judge, by complex and diversified mental qualities and conditions. Of these the most important have been: the love of science, unbounded patience in long reflecting over any subject, industry in observing and collecting facts, and a fair share of invention as well as of commonsense. With such moderate abilities as I possess, it is truly surprising that thus I should have influenced to a considerable extent the beliefs of scientific men on some important points.

If I lived twenty years more and was able to work, how I should modify the *Origin,* and how much the views on all points will have to be modified! Well, it is a beginning, and that is something. . . .
Letter from Charles Darwin to J. D. Hooker, 1869.

Acknowledgements

Pictures are listed from top to bottom of the page

Picture research by Naomi Narod

Map by Gordon Cramp Studio

page 31 Reproduced by kind permission of the Syndics of the Cambridge University Library
49 E. Hummel/ZEFA
50 all H. Eisenbeiss
51 *left* J. K. Burras/Oxford Scientific Films; E. S. Ross; D. Philcox
right E. S. Ross; E. S. Ross; J. K. Burras /Oxford Scientific Films
52 K. Weidmann/Oxford Scientific Films/Animals, Animals
53 *left* H. Rivarola/Bruce Coleman Ltd; Stephen Dalton/NHPA; E. S. Ross
right G. I. Bernard/Oxford Scientific Films; E. S. Ross; E. S. Ross; Stephen Dalton/NHPA
54 both H. Rivarola/Bruce Coleman Ltd
55 *left* H. Rivarola/Bruce Coleman Ltd; E. S. Ross; E. S. Ross
right all E. S. Ross
56 *left* Franz Lazi; H. Rivarola/Bruce Coleman Ltd
right E. S. Ross; Oxford Scientific Films
73 Nino Cirani/SALMER
74 Loren McIntyre; Francisco Erize/Bruce Coleman Ltd; Francisco Erize/Bruce Coleman Ltd
75 H. Rivarola/Bruce Coleman Ltd; Francisco Erize/Bruce Coleman Ltd
76 Tony Morrison; Des & Jen Bartlett/Bruce Coleman Ltd; Gary Milburn/Tom Stack & Associates
101 B. N. Kelly; Loren McIntyre
102 B. N. Kelly
103 SALMER; Loren McIntyre
104 *left* Tony Morrison; RTHPL
right Royal Geographical Society/photo John Freeman
125 Nino Cirani/SALMER
126 Gary Milburn/Tom Stack & Associates
127 Loren McIntyre
128 Eric Crichton/Bruce Coleman Ltd; Loren McIntyre
145 B. N. Kelly
146 Anthony Huxley
147 Heather Angel
148 *left* M. P. Harris/Bruce Coleman Ltd; M. P. Harris; M. P. Harris; M. P. Harris/Bruce Coleman Ltd

148 *right* M. P. Harris/Bruce Coleman Ltd; rest M. P. Harris
149 Francisco Erize/Bruce Coleman Ltd; Heather Angel
150 Norman Tomalin/Bruce Coleman Ltd
151 *left* Heather Angel; Michael & Barbara Reed/Oxford Scientific Films/ Animals, Animals; Michael & Barbara Reed/Oxford Scientific Films/ Animals, Animals
right Heather Angel; Anthony Huxley; Duncan M. Porter; Duncan M. Porter
152 Francisco Erize/Bruce Coleman Ltd; Heather Angel
159 Mitchell Library, Sydney

NOTE

In the index that follows entries are made principally under the names that Darwin used. Sometimes these names have changed since his day (see e.g. *Athene cunicularia, Diodon antennatus*), and sometimes Darwin himself made mistakes – for example, what he calls the Agouti is really the Mara, or Patagonian Cavy (the true Agouti is a different animal from northern South America). Similarly, in speaking of Batrachian 'reptiles' Darwin confuses the group of frogs, toads, newts etc (Batrachians) with that of lizards, snakes, turtles etc (reptiles). In such cases the anomalous terms used by Darwin are here printed with single quotation marks.

Index of flora and fauna mentioned on the Voyage

Figures in *italics* refer to illustrations